Neural Path
THERAPY

HOW TO CHANGE
YOUR BRAIN'S RESPONSE TO
ANGER, FEAR, PAIN & DESIRE

MATTHEW M^cKAY, PH.D.
DAVID HARP, MA

NEW HARBINGER PUBLICATIONS, INC.

Publisher's Note

Some of the concepts contained in this book are also proprietary titles or main components of coauthor David Harp's corporate presentations, including Mental Muscle™, Neural Path Therapy™, NPT™, Neural Navigation™, Self-Therapeutic Tools™, The Draw A Breath Chart™, Nervous? It's Just Your Nervous System!™, The R n' R Response™, The Emotion Equation™, How to See It Coming, Before It Hits the Fan™, Progressive Neural Desensitization™, and PND™. Many of the compassion and softening around pain exercises in steps three and four are based on those in The Three Minute Meditator, *used with the kind permission of the coauthor of that book, Dr. Nina Smiley. All diagrams and illustrations are © David Harp, 2005.*

This publication is designed to provide accurate and authoritative information in regard to the subject matter covered. It is sold with the understanding that the publisher is not engaged in rendering psychological, financial, legal, or other professional services. If expert assistance or counseling is needed, the services of a competent professional should be sought.

Note: If you are in a lot of physical or mental pain, it may be wise—and compassionate to yourself—to read this entire book before starting to work with the real-life exercises in step one. Just read about it, think about it (especially about the sections on compassion and on softening around pain), but don't try to use the program until you really feel ready.

Distributed in Canada by Raincoast Books.

New Harbinger Publications, Inc.
5674 Shattuck Avenue
Oakland, CA 94609

Cover design by Amy Shoup
Text design by Michele Waters-Kermes
Acquired by Tesilya Hanauer
Edited by Brady Kahn

ISBN 1-57224-426-7 Paperback

Printed in the United States of America

New Harbinger Publications' Web site address: www.newharbinger.com

Library of Congress Cataloging-in-Publication Data

McKay, Matthew.
  Neural path therapy : how to change your brain's response to anger, fear, pain, and
desire / Matthew McKay and David Harp.
      p. cm.
  Includes bibliographical references.
  ISBN 1-57224-426-7
  1. Cognitive therapy. 2. Stress management. 3. Neural networks (Neurobiology)
I. Harp, David. II. Title.
  RC489.C63M33 2005
  616.89'142—dc22
                                        2005014371
07 06 05

10 9 8 7 6 5 4 3 2 1

First printing

For all my clients, past and present, who've taught me so much about life and our potential for change.
—M.M.

I dedicate this book to my beloved twin sister, Dr. Nina Smiley, and her husband Bert Smiley, of Mohonk Mountain House, Lake Mohonk, New York.
—D.H.

Contents

Preface

Neural Path Therapy is a five-step self-help method that trains the user in a new form of cognitive behavioral therapy, or CBT. CBT is currently considered to be the fastest and most effective form of therapy and the only nondrug therapy that has been experimentally proven to work.

This book combines the clinical knowledge of one of the nation's most experienced cognitive behavioral therapists, Matthew McKay, Ph.D., with the state-of-the-art presentation style of cognitive scientist and corporate presenter David Harp. It has been created as a resource for readers, whether they are in or out of therapy. We hope and believe that therapists may also find it of value, for using with their clients, and perhaps for using themselves.

MATTHEW'S STORY

I'm Matthew McKay. I want to start by welcoming you to our book. We wrote it for you because David and I have both struggled at times with big, overwhelming emotions. And we have discovered new ways to cope that, I believe, could change your life.

When I was young I was plagued by fear—of being alone, of rejection, of being far from home, of failure. Fear controlled my life, tremendously limiting what I could risk or achieve. Standard psychodynamic therapies failed me. They offered insights without real tools for change. Then, in graduate school, I discovered cognitive behavioral therapy.

CBT gave me something I had never possessed before—real skills for coping with fear. I learned effective relaxation techniques. I learned to confront and change my fear-evoking thoughts. I learned to gradually expose myself to frightening situations so that I stopped avoiding them. But most of all, CBT taught me that I had the power to change, to get better. I had been given tools that I could carry with me forever.

This is important. Instead of the power to change residing with a therapist, it was inside of me. And it was available, day or night, whenever I needed it. Whenever I was anxious or scared, I had confidence in my ability to manage my feelings without getting overwhelmed.

Now let's fast-forward. I have been a psychologist for twenty-seven years. In that time I have treated more than five hundred clients and supervised ninety interns. What I've come to realize is that CBT, though tremendously helpful and effective, has limitations. It's hard for people to talk back to their negative thoughts; it's hard to dispute damaging beliefs. There are a lot of people who simply can't or won't do it. And there are others who, initially successful, give up the effort and slide back to their pain.

That's why David and I felt the need to develop new tools and a broader approach to consciousness change. Neural path therapy doesn't replace CBT, but it provides new, powerful skills for altering the direction of our thoughts and, ultimately, for changing chronic, painful emotional reactions.

David and I have been friends and colleagues for more than twenty years. This collaboration grows from our longtime quest to meld the ancient disciplines of transformation with brain science and modern technologies of change. Neural path therapy works, and it is now our pleasure to give the tools we've found to you.

DAVID'S STORY

Hi. I'm David Harp. I can sum up the purpose of this book, and the mission of my life for the past twenty years, in a few words.

> THE BETTER YOU UNDERSTAND A TOOL,
> THE BETTER YOU CAN USE IT.
> AND YOUR BRAIN IS THE BEST TOOL YOU'LL EVER HAVE.

I never planned to become a cognitive psychologist—that is, a scientist who studies how the processes of the brain influence our every emotion and action. Rather, I was forced to learn to understand my own brain because I had such a difficult one. Since childhood, I'd been plagued by insecurity and obsessive fears, lots of anger, and an inability to stay focused on anything that did not provide an immediate reward. So my life was a mess, no matter how dramatic or entertaining I might have appeared to others.

The story of my transformation from a vain, wretched, manipulative young man to a reasonably happy if mildly neurotic husband, father, prolific writer, and corporate speaker has been detailed elsewhere (Harp 1996).

My tale of woe and change is unimportant. What is relevant is this: If you are troubled by fear or anger, if you sometimes speak or act in ways that don't, on reflection, serve you well, if you feel empty or lonely, then you need to learn to understand and control that mysterious and often mutinous creature known as the human brain.

For two and a half decades, I've studied that strange creature, at psychology clinics and suicide hotlines, at meditation retreats and in hospice settings. And in hundreds of presentations for clients ranging from Ben & Jerry's to the Red Cross, from Kraft Foods to Merck Pharmaceutical, from Paul Newman's camps for sick kids to the FBI, I've taught tens of thousands of people to use their greatest tool more effectively. By doing so, they gain skills for living and working and loving with better communication, more compassion, and less anxiety, anger, and stress.

My way of teaching may seem strange to some—I use the humble vehicle of the blues harmonica to allow my audiences to demonstrate for themselves the most crucial lessons of cognitive psychology. Strange, yes—but it works. I've honed my methods to the degree that I can now face the challenge of training those who must have the ability to function well in tense situations: forensic groups, crisis-response groups, hospice groups. And it has not escaped me that most of us, regardless of our type of employment, have great need of this same ability. So I'm honored to have the opportunity to present my work to you, dear reader, in conjunction with my friend, mentor, and former clinical supervisor, Dr. Matthew McKay.

WHY WE WROTE THIS BOOK

We came together to write this book from two very different directions. But we are in complete agreement on both the scientific methods underlying this book and the book's purpose.

Matthew is a highly experienced psychotherapist, using cognitive behavioral therapy to help his clients explore and work with their thoughts. David has studied mindfulness-based self-help methods for nearly two decades and is a nationally acclaimed corporate speaker who enlightens and motivates his audiences with a mind-boggling combination of harmonica and cognitive science.

Our career paths have been quite dissimilar. Matthew's interest is more in the realm of thoughts—helping his clients to understand them, manipulate them, use them to advantage. David is more interested in physiological reactions, words, and actions and interactions in the workplace, as well as in the spiritual implications and uses of mindfulness. But we both believe, with great passion, that understanding your mind is the first step to making your life more manageable and satisfying.

We also believe that our current activities—psychotherapy and corporate presentations—fall short of what we'd like to do. We asked ourselves, "How can we reach out to help people when they are not sitting in front of us?"

Our answer was to combine our areas of expertise and create a five-step method based on David's presentations and Matthew's therapeutic experience. This method will teach you how to act as your own therapist, whether you have a professional therapist or not.

THE GOAL OF THIS BOOK

This book is here to help you

- Put yourself in conscious control of your moods

- Reverse harmful stress reactions

- Handle anger, fear, and desire

- Change outdated or negative emotional habits

- Have confidence that you can cope with *whatever* comes up

This book will train you, in a few simple lessons, to carry your own skills with you. Wherever you go. Whenever you need them. You won't have to be sitting on a therapist's couch to be "therapeutized." You won't need to listen to a motivational speaker to be motivated. In short, we'll give you five simple steps to help you cope with just about anything.

IS THIS BOOK FOR YOU?

Imagine that you could choose to have a lifelong relationship with one of two people. The first is with a tyrant, who alternates between slyly betraying you and berating and bullying you for your inadequacies. A cross between the meanest kid in your high school and Mr. Dithers, the despotic boss in the *Blondie* comic strip.

The second is with a wonderful, creative servant. A cross between Aladdin's genie ("Your wish is my command, O Master!") and the best friend you could ever imagine.

Which relationship would you choose?

You're no fool. Of course you'd choose the latter. And yet, for many of us, our relationship with our own brain and mind is more like the former. If you are ready to change the way in which you interact with your own mind—the most important relationship you have—read on.

HOW TO USE THIS BOOK

As you might expect from a book written by a therapist and an ex-therapist, we tend to think that just about anyone can benefit from psychotherapy, at least during the rough spots that life tends to put you through. But if you are not in therapy, our method may be especially valuable for you. It may also be used to great effect in conjunction with a program of individual therapy.

Turbocharge Your Therapy

If you are currently seeing a therapist, this book will have two main purposes:

- You can use it when you're not in your therapist's office (during the week between therapy sessions) and during difficult events or when difficult emotions arise.

- It will teach you the cognitive skills that allow you to get the most out of your therapy—anywhere, anytime—and thus the most out of your life.

If You Are Not Seeing a Therapist

This book will give you the tools to act as your own therapist.

- It will start by providing you with insight, just as a good therapist might, into how the brain works. You'll then begin learning a variety of self-therapeutic tools.

- While you practice using these tools, we'll give you specific instruction on how to identify and understand the types of emotional issues that a therapist might help you deal with.

- You'll then start applying the tools to the issues, thus conducting your own therapy.

Use It with a Friend or a Group

It can be more fun and very effective to do some of the exercises in this book as "duets" or in a small group. Do you have a friend or coworker who is interested in self-help, stress reduction, or having a more creative life? If so, please read about our Web site (see the back of the book) for more information on using this book with a friend or with a group.

A Message to Therapists

If you are a therapist reading this book, please visit our Web site and see our comments on using this book with clients (see the back of the book).

THE STAKES ARE HIGH, SO BE DILIGENT

We are confident that our method works—but it only works if you use it. So give this book a sincere try for at least a week—devoting, say, ten or fifteen minutes a day to reading it and another ten or fifteen minutes to practicing the various exercises. It may sound like a significant investment of time, but your happiness and mental health for the rest of your life could depend on it.

A warning: Please don't let doubt or skepticism undercut your initial efforts. Every human being has the ability to change and grow. This is true whether you believe it or not. So you must either believe it—or act as though you do—and commit yourself to giving it a fair try.

Acknowledgments

I'd like to begin by acknowledging the debt I owe to my professors at Wesleyan University: Karl Scheibe, Lincoln Keiser, the late Robert Knapp, and Vito Modigliani (whose psycho-physiology class gave me my first view of those crucial building blocks, the axons and dendrites of the human brain). And continue by thanking my professors at Sonoma State University: Art Warmoth, Nina Menrath, Larry Horowitz, and Frank Siroky. I will never forget my gratitude to those who have helped me wrestle with philosophic, religious, and spiritual issues: Stephen and Ondrea Levine, and Jack Kornfield (whose patience I surely tried in our weekly "spiritual counseling" sessions).

Nor the counselors who provided training, therapy, and role models: Charles Garfield, Stephen Bank, and David Brosell. I'd also like to thank friends like Tom Liebermann and his delightful family, who were so instrumental in my becoming a corporate speaker, Justin Morreale for his ongoing faith in my writing, and

Larry Adelman, Sal Bellia, Al Bernstein, Don Canestro, and John Meharg for the great gift of their friendship. And my co-author Matthew McKay, who after a quarter of a century still astonishes me with his diversity of talent. Plus, of course, my wife and partner Rita Ricketson, who has both played an indispensable role in helping me to develop every aspect of my career and our business, and even more importantly, collaborated with me in producing two of my most favorite human beings in the whole world: Lily, and Katie.

—David Harp, 2005

Introduction

Neural path therapy (NPT) is the self-help method that David created in 1999 and has honed in more than a hundred group trainings involving well over ten thousand participants. Neural path therapy is based on three main concepts:

- Mental muscle

- Neural paths

- The relax-and-release (R & R) response

Over the next five chapters, you'll learn the five steps that will allow you to, as we like to say, "calm down and cope with just about anything." These are

- The Power of the Breath: A Little R & R

- Thought Watching: Your Neural Neighborhood

- Compassion: Healing the Hurt Spots

- Softening Around Pain: When Life Is Hard

- Wise Paths: Putting It All Together

In chapter 6, you'll explore what we call "The Path to Total Freedom." Here we'll discuss the spiritual implications of the NPT method, in case you are interested. Whether or not you are, this method will work for you.

For now, the three main concepts—mental muscle, neural paths, and the R & R response—are what you need to understand, so in the following pages, we'll make each of them simple to understand and easy to use. And we won't just describe these elements. Rather, we'll let you demonstrate each concept for yourself.

MENTAL MUSCLE

Consider physical muscle. With the exception of bodybuilders, most people use physical exercise to develop muscles so they can *use* them. There are lots of situations that require muscle: sports that use muscle range from tennis to kayaking to kickboxing. Workplace usage of muscle might range from doing Antarctic ecological field research on skis to walking a mail route to being a bouncer at a bar. But the basic exercises needed to build muscle—like running, calisthenics, and weight lifting—are the same, no matter what the end use of that muscle might be.

Similarly, you're going to build mental muscle—not just so your brain will look impressive in a bathing suit, but to use it to enhance your existence. The basic exercises used to build mental muscle are simple and relatively few in number. But the uses to which you can apply mental muscle are as varied as the situations that arise in your own life.

We'll define mental muscle in a moment. However, before doing that, we'd like you to demonstrate its use for yourself.

The Mental Muscle Experiment

Here's a little experiment to show how mental muscle works. Please do the following exercise before reading further.

Guess how thick this book is.
Half an inch? A centimeter?
Whisper your answer to yourself.
Now guess how much the book weighs.
A pound? 5 ounces? 200 grams?
Again, whisper your answer.

The Average Person Versus the Cognitive Scientist

How did you answer these questions? You might say that you looked at the spine, made a guess as to how thick it was, and whispered your answer. Then you hefted the book in your hand, guessed at its weight, and again whispered the answer to yourself. This is how the average person would describe what he or she did.

As cognitive scientists, we'd describe what happened in terms of a series of three actions: perceiving, processing, and outputting.

You began by focusing the power of your brain through your eyes onto the spine of the book. You perceived the thickness of that spine with your sense of sight. You then processed that perception by comparing it to your knowledge of size, in inches or centimeters. And you ended by outputting your answer in the form of whispered words.

Then you shifted the power of your brain away from your eyes (most people will look away from the book when they attempt to guess its weight—did you?). You sent the power of your brain down the nerves of your spine and arm, into your hand, where your sense of touch perceived the gravitational pull of the book. You then processed that perception by comparing it to your knowledge of weight, in ounces, pounds, or grams. Finally, you outputted your answer in a few whispered words.

MENTAL MUSCLE IS SIMPLY THE ABILITY TO FOCUS THE POWER OF YOUR BRAIN WHERE YOU WANT IT, WHEN YOU WANT IT.

IT'S EASY TO DO—IF YOU ARE FOCUSING ON PHYSICAL OBJECTS, LIKE THIS BOOK.

UNFORTUNATELY, MOST OF US HAVE NEVER BEEN TAUGHT HOW TO FOCUS—OR NOT FOCUS—ON MENTAL OBJECTS, LIKE THOUGHTS, EMOTIONS, OR MENTAL PATHWAYS.

Shifting Attention: So What?

Of course you can look at a book, then shift your mental attention to weigh it in your hand. Of course you can read these words, then shift the focus of your attention to look up at the clock. We have all learned, from childhood, to focus our attention with ease on physical objects like books, or clocks, or harmonicas—and to change the focus of our attention at will, from one thing to another.

Do you need mental muscle? Answer the following questions to find out:

- Are you ever troubled by fear, anger, or repetitive thoughts?

- Do you ever find yourself worrying about whether you'll meet the deadline rather than staying focused on the deadline task?

- Do you worry about the impression that you're making on people rather than simply being yourself?

If, like most of us, you suffer from these problems, you may never have developed the type of mental muscle that you really need. But we'll give you exercises to help build up this crucial but neglected aspect of your mental musculature. And then you'll use that muscle to observe and navigate neural paths.

PATHWAYS IN THE BRAIN

Nerve cells, or neurons, are long, narrow cells found in nerve tissue throughout the body. But most of them—about 100 billion—compose the gray matter of the human brain. You can think of each neuron as a small device for transmitting electrical, chemical, or hormonal information from one end of the neuron to the other. The *dendrites* receive information and transmit that information to the cell body. The *axon* takes information away from the cell body. So the information travels from dendrite end to axon end of the neuron.

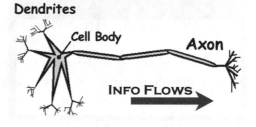

A single neuron can't transmit information very far. But fortunately, neurons can connect together, axon to dendrite, to form what are called *neural paths* (or *neural chains* or *neural networks*). Every time we learn to perform a new action or think a new thought, a string of neurons connects together, end to end, to form a brand new neural path.

So write the nonsense word *amthagor* in cursive script, or think of Martians visiting your favorite restaurant, and presto: you've created a new neural path for yourself.

Why is this important? Well, if neurons are the building blocks of your brain, then the pathways they form are the building blocks of your mind and of your personailty. Thus neural pathways have a tremendous effect on your thoughts, your emotions, and your actions.

First Commitment: Drawing a Breath

You will probably be able to get the idea of neural paths better if you demonstrate it for yourself. So we will now ask you to do something that may seem silly or irrelevant—learning to use the draw-a-breath chart. We guarantee that you'll put it to good use very soon.

This is your first lesson in diligence—in committing yourself to the neural path therapy program. We humbly beg you to give us two or three minutes of your most careful attention here, to demonstrate a really important element of this method.

The Ins and Outs of Breathing

Consider breathing. Each breath can be composed of three actions:

- Inhaling (breathing in)

- Exhaling (breathing out)

- Holding (a space of *any* length between in- and out-breaths)

1. Practice for a breath or two, noticing each component of the breath: innn–hold–oouut. Notice that often the hold between breaths is so short—a fraction of a second when you are breathing neither in nor out—it's almost nonexistent: in–hold–out.

2. Try a few faster, shallower (less full) breaths: in–hold–out–hold–in–hold–out.

3. Try a deeper breath, and put a one or two second hold after the exhale:
    innnnnnn … hold … ooouuut … hooold … innnnnn.

The Draw-a-Breath Chart

The draw-a-breath chart is a simple, visual way of describing a breathing pattern. Three lines represent the three actions of the breath (inhaling, exhaling, and holding).

- A black line that slants up represents an inhale. The higher the line goes, the deeper the inhale. When the line hits the top gray bar, your lungs are comfortably full.

- A black line that slants down represents an exhale. The lower the line goes, the more complete your exhale. When an exhale line hits the lower gray bar, your lungs will be comfortably empty.

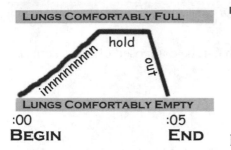

LUNGS COMFORTABLY FULL

hold

out

innnnnnnnnn

LUNGS COMFORTABLY EMPTY

:00   :05
BEGIN   **END**

■ A horizontal (flat) black line represents holding the breath. You can hold your breath no matter how full or empty your lungs are.

You read the chart from left to right. Moving from left to right represents the passage of time. The steeper the line, the faster the breath (whether inhale or exhale).

Try reading this simplified diagram at left, which charts out one breath, taking about five seconds to complete it.

Did you read the chart correctly? This particular breath:

1. Starts empty and fills up slowly (a line begins at the bottom and gradually slants up to the lungs-full bar; the caption reads "innnnnnnnnn").

2. Holds for a second when full (across a short flat line near the top gray bar; the caption reads "hold").

3. Then exhales rapidly (down the sharply slanting line to the bottom gray bar; the caption reads "out").

You'll use the draw-a-breath chart in two important ways. It will give you an object lesson in how neural paths develop. And it will help you to build mental muscle.

Breathing with the Chart

This next draw-a-breath chart is more complicated and represents about half a minute (five breaths) worth of breathing. There's nothing special about this particular pattern—just an example, for experimental purposes. And you're about to be your own test subject!

To breathe along with the chart below, start out at the left, with your lungs comfortably empty (the line starts down low). Then take three relatively slow breaths, starting on the inhale, with a short hold in between each inhale and exhale. On the chart, each "innnnnn ... hold ... ooouuut" represents a single slow breath.

The third slow breath is shallower than the first two: you start with your lungs empty, but inhale more slowly and only fill your lungs halfway before holding and exhaling. This is represented by the "hold" line being midway between the upper gray bar (lungs comfortably full) and the lower gray bar (lungs comfortably empty).

Then you finish with two faster breaths (the two pointy in–out in–out ones) without any holds between inhale and exhale. These last two are full breaths. At the end of the second faster breath, your lungs should be fairly empty.

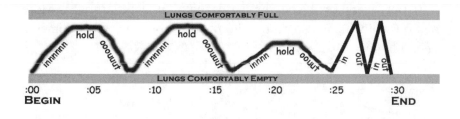

Please try to breathe along with this chart two or three times *before* going on to the next section. You can breathe through your nose or your mouth. It doesn't matter if you don't take exactly the same amount of time as written—don't bother to look at your watch as you do this.

Just try to get the general feel of approximating a breathing pattern: in this case, "innnnnn ... hold ... ooouuut ... innnnnn ... hold ... ooouuut ... innnn ... hold ... oouut ... in ... out ... in ... out"

STRENGTHENING YOUR NEURAL PATHS

If you're like most people, the first time you tried to mimic the breathing pattern above, it seemed a bit confusing. After doing it two or three times, it was much easier. Why did it get easier? The obvious answer, of course, is practice. But a cognitive scientist would tell you that when your brain connects up those neurons that create a neural path, it's a thin, weak, wimpy path, at first:

But every time you reuse this path, it gets stronger. More neurons join in, and a thin, wimpy string of neurons becomes a neural highway:

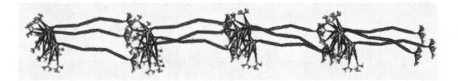

Imagine renting a cabin on a lake. The first time you walk from the cabin door to the fishing dock, you have to fight your way through chest-high grass and weeds. What a mess! But as you return from the dock to the cabin, it's a bit easier—you've stomped down a bit of a path. By the end of the week, after walking back and forth a few dozen times a day, you've got a nice, wide thoroughfare from cabin to dock.

Neural paths work much the same way. The more you use them, the easier they are to use—wider, stronger, more robust.

And if you stop using them, they tend to fade out, just as the cabin to dock path would get overgrown if you stopped walking it.

Perceive, Process, and Output

Many pathways follow a perceive → process → output formula. We described this same formula earlier when discussing mental muscle.

- You perceive information using your senses (as in seeing or feeling the book).

- You process that information in some way (comparing the sight or weight with other sizing and weighing information that you already know).

- You output an action of some kind (such as whispering the thickness or weight of the book to yourself).

As you learned to breathe along with the draw-a-breath chart, you created a neural pathway that followed this general perceive → process → output pattern. The following diagram illustrates the "learning to read the draw-a-breath chart" neural path. Remember, each time you follow this neural path, more neurons join in, and the path grows stronger. That's why it gets easier.

Hardwired Neural Paths

Although most neural paths follow this perceive → process → output formula, there are a few variations on the basic theme. Of these variations, the most important are what we might call hardwired, or automatic, paths. These are neural paths that are built right into the brain and activate automatically when you perceive certain events. The brain in question might be in a bug, a frog, a dog, or even a human being. For example, the frog's brain is wired so that when the frog perceives a small flying object, that visual information is automatically and instantly processed (hardwired), and an action is outputted: the frog's tongue snaps out to nail the bug!

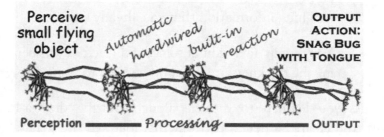

Perceive small flying object *Automatic hardwired built-in reaction* **OUTPUT ACTION: SNAG BUG WITH TONGUE**

Perception ———— *Processing* ———— **OUTPUT**

ONCE YOU BECOME AWARE OF THESE PATHWAYS, BOTH IN GENERAL (HOW NEURAL PATHWAYS WORK) AND SPECIFICALLY (WHAT YOURS ARE AND WHERE THEY LEAD YOU), YOU CAN BEGIN TO OBSERVE THEM.

AFTER OBSERVING THEM, YOU CAN CHANGE THEM, LET THEM FALL INTO DISUSE, OR CREATE NEW ONES, SO THAT YOU NO LONGER HABITUALLY FOLLOW MENTAL PATHWAYS THAT MAY HAVE BEEN ORIGINALLY CREATED BY WHIM, ACCIDENT, OR FOR REASONS WHICH ARE NO LONGER APPROPRIATE!

Neural Navigation

This whole neural path business would just be an interesting bit of trivia if it were not for the fact that a great deal of your emotional life is controlled by these silly little chains of neurons. In the next chapters, you'll see how they can have a profound effect on anger and fear, relationships and love, work habits, desires, and almost every aspect of your life.

As we've said, the brain and mind can act as either a despotic master or a wonderful servant. When you learn to observe and control its processes, *you* become the master, and your brain and mind are relegated to the useful, creative, support roles that they were meant to serve. However, if you want this to happen, you must first learn to override two hardwired neural paths. So it's time to take a brief look at the human nervous system.

NERVOUS? IT'S JUST YOUR NERVOUS SYSTEM!

Now that you understand mental muscle and neural paths, it's time to explain the third and last theoretical concept of the neural path therapy method: the *relax-and-release response.*

This hardwired response is created by a particular part of your *nervous system,* a term that refers to all of the nerve cells in the body. The nervous system is made up of a number of parts with scary sounding names. But all you really need to know is this: the relax-and-release response and its equal but opposite partner, the fight-or-flight response, are hardwired into your neural paths, and they affect almost every aspect of your life.

> THE WHOLE POINT OF THE FIGHT-OR-FLIGHT
> RESPONSE IS TO STIMULATE FEAR AND ANGER—FEAR
> TO HELP YOU FLEE, ANGER TO HELP YOU FIGHT. BOTH
> ARE USEFUL RESPONSES IN THE APPROPRIATE
> SITUATION. IF TRIGGERED INAPPROPRIATELY, THEY
> CAN MAKE YOUR LIFE MISERABLE.

The Fight-or-Flight Response

One part of your nervous system, the sympathetic nervous system, is hardwired to produce the fight-or-flight response. When the fight-or-flight response is triggered, a storm of chemical, electrical, and hormonal changes rack your entire body.

Here's what happens:

- Your digestion stops (so that all of your energy can go to fighting or fleeing).

- Blood rushes from your extremities to the core of your body (so that when the saber-toothed tiger attacks, you don't bleed out and can whack him with your stone axe while he chews your other hand).

- Adrenaline and other hormones and chemicals flood your brain.

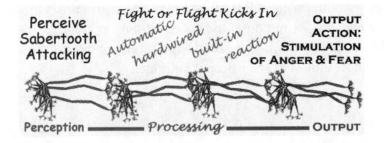

The Relax-and-Release Response

Another part of your nervous system, the parasympathetic nervous system, is hardwired to do the job of returning your body to normal once the crisis is over. In other words, it counters the effects of the fight-or-flight response.

This relax-and-release response (or R & R response), like the fight-or-flight response, is hardwired into the brain. At some point—after the crisis is over, after the saber-toothed cat has been fought off—your parasympathetic nervous system will kick in, to undo the fight-or-flight response. Blood will return to your extremities, digestion will start up again, your pulse rate will come back to normal. Your brain tells your body, "Relax. The danger is past." You can feel it happen, and you may sigh, say "phew!" and drop your shoulders—that's the release part.

A Useful Path ... Sometimes

When events render fast action necessary, this entire process can be worth its weight in HMO bills. For example, when that taxi jumps the curb and is heading straight for you, do you engage in lots of analysis or self-talk? ("Let's see, there's been news of a taxi strike; maybe this has something to do with that. Or, hmmm, could it be my 'Surrounded by Idiots' T-shirt?")

Of course, you don't try to *think* it through—you'd be roadkill before you could go through half of that! Instead, your good old hardwired fight-or-flight response kicks in, and you leap to safety without so much as a hint of a thought. Sooner or later, after you've picked yourself out of the gutter, your heart rate subsides, your muscles relax, and you're ready to go on with your life. The following diagram shows the neural path of this process:

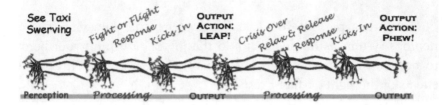

But in many, many circumstances of modern life, the fight-or-flight response does more damage than good. It may not be obvious, but it is the power behind the scene—the biological mechanism that brings anger, fear, desire, envy, jealousy, and other negative emotions into your life.

Hidden Hardwiring That Controls Your Life

It's almost impossible to avoid noticing the fight-or-flight response once it gets triggered. But controlling it, on the other hand, probably seems just about impossible—like controlling a hurricane or an earthquake. And most of us are not even aware that the relax-and-release response exists. When it kicks in, we just say "phew!"—and are glad that the crisis or upset is over.

Yet for reasons that will become clear as you read on, learning to gain conscious control over these two crucial responses is the key to coping with just about anything. Because if you can't control them, they will control you!

> LEARNING HOW TO USE MENTAL MUSCLE AND NEURAL PATHS TO CONSCIOUSLY TRIGGER THE RELAX-AND-RELEASE RESPONSE MAY BECOME THE MOST USEFUL THING THAT YOU KNOW HOW TO DO.

In the next chapter, we'll investigate ways to overrule the two main hardwired pathways of the human brain. You'll begin to learn how use mental muscle to avoid unnecessarily stimulating the fight-or-flight response and how to trigger the relax-and-release response—at will.

CHAPTER 1

Step One

The Power of the Breath: A Little R & R

Let's take a quick look at the basic concepts that we covered in the introduction.

- Mental muscle is the ability to focus the power of the brain where you want it, when you want it. Most of us are very good at focusing on—or turning our attention away from—physical objects and not so good at focusing on mental objects like thoughts, emotions, or neural paths.

- Neural paths provide a simple way to visualize processes in the brain. Probably the most important aspect of neural paths is that—like most paths— they get bigger and easier to follow the more you use them.

- Two powerful responses are hardwired into some of your neural paths. The fight-or-flight response readies you, instantly, to flee or do combat. The more subtle but equally important relax-and-release response reverses the effects of the fight-or-flight response.

The following chapter covers step one—the essential core of the neural path therapy method. It is broken into three main parts. In the first part, you'll learn how thoughts can trigger the fight-or-fight response and what to do about that. In the second part, we'll present breathing exercises to suit every taste and situation. In the third part, you'll change an established neural path—by consciously stimulating your own R & R response—in a real-life situation. Once you've begun to master step one, the rest of this book will teach you to hone and refine your ability to use it to calm down and cope with just about anything.

A POKE WITH A PIN

Poke an amoeba or your pet pig with a pin, and you can prove to yourself that all living creatures are hardwired so that perception of an event can trigger the fight-or-flight response. And it's not difficult to understand, from experience, how eventually (and unconsciously) the relax-and-release response kicks in once the crisis is over. But only human beings can trigger this awesome chain of physiological events with a mere thought!

The Least Favorite Person Exercise

Imagine, for a moment, your least favorite person in the world, whether it be an ex-lover from Hades or an unscrupulous politician, the car salesman who sold you that lemon or a frightening terrorist. If you *really* hate or fear this individual, you'll more than likely notice that you have a physical reaction to his or her image as it appears in your mind.

Perhaps you experience a tightening sensation, a clenching of teeth or hands (the better to bite or choke you with, our primitive ancestors might say) as anger arises, or perhaps butterflies in your stomach, shallow breathing, a chill up the back—if the image brings fear. Either way, you've just demonstrated for yourself that a mere phantasm in the mind—a thought—can trigger the fight-or-flight response, resulting in anger or fear.

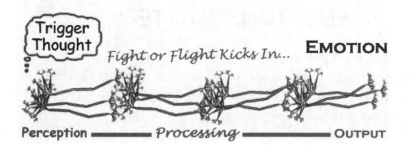

We can sum up this sequence of events, from trigger thought to fear or anger, with what we call the emotion equation. An emotion is produced by a thought or event that triggers a fight-or-flight response.

THE EMOTION EQUATION:

THOUGHT OR EVENT + FIGHT-OR-FLIGHT RESPONSE = EMOTION

It doesn't matter whether the response is triggered by a mental event (a thought) or a physical event—the fight-or-flight response is the same. It doesn't matter whether the triggering thought or event has any intrinsic fear or anger potential. For example, imagine watching someone catch a butterfly. If you are a fanatical and competitive butterfly collector, the thought of a rival netting a lovely specimen of *Erikssonia acraeina* might drive you mad with jealousy. But the same thought (or the actual event) would mean nothing to a collector of antique gas station signs. What's the difference? For the sign collector, that thought or event does not stimulate the fight-or-flight response, so the thought remains just a thought, and the event remains just something that has been perceived.

WHY EMOTIONS MATTER

It's not hard to make the case that some neural paths leading to a fight-or-flight response are useful or even essential (like the out-of-control-taxi-leap-to-safety neural path in the introduction). Unfortunately, many neural paths that begin with a trigger thought are unhelpful, overused, and even unhealthy. This is because the fight-or-flight response is tough on the body—it is a desperate measure, meant to be used rarely and in case of actual emergency. It's not meant to be stimulated on a daily basis, caused by nothing more real than an image in the mind. You might imagine your boss approaching—pink slip in hand—and get a cold chill down your spine every single time you see or think of her. That's like taking a course of antibiotics eight times a month, every time you worry that you might have encountered a germ.

Some of us can replay the same negative fear or anger trigger thought a dozen or more times a day. But remember, please, the practice effect—that neural paths are strengthened by repeated use. Each time you activate the path (with the trigger thought), you make it stronger, wider, and more likely to be activated yet again. In addition, the more you practice a path (on purpose or not)—the *faster* you progress along it.

Too Swift to See: Automaticity

When you have a favorite fear or anger thought, the neural path often becomes so well trodden that the entire processing part, between trigger thought and fight-or-flight response, happens so quickly that it is almost imperceptible, virtually automated. For example, one of our clients has a tendency to ruminate (think over and over) about a particular business acquaintance whose image instantly raises the fight part of the fight-or-flight response. Another tends to indulge in worrying about his adolescent child, in which the merest thought of a driver's permit—or even a car that reminds him of his teenager's vehicle—catapults fear into his mind.

This instant processing effect is called *automaticity*. Once a neural path is this well developed, it can be hard even to notice its existence: "Oh," you say, "I think of _____ and I just go ballistic." In a very real way, automaticity is like turning the process part of a neural path into a hardwired reaction. This can be useful when you learn to create positive neural paths and make them automatic. More commonly, however, it works against people, as they create a convenient shortcut from trigger thought or trigger event to instant anger or fear.

We'll discuss the subtleties of learning to watch, evaluate, and control your own neural paths in step two. But now, it's time to learn how to short-circuit the fight-or-flight response and to build the mental muscle that will let you do so in a real-life situation.

Reading About It Is Not Enough

Clearly, any fool can trigger a fight-or-flight response at the drop of a hat—or an insult, real or perceived—and many do. In fact, you don't need to be a fool to do it, since most of us habitually host negative thoughts that give rise to habitual negative emotions or actions. Unfortunately, simply understanding the emotion equation isn't enough. It's up to you to learn how to reverse, or short-circuit, the fight-or-flight response. Doing this is a crucial element of neural path therapy, for unless the fight-or-flight response is triggered, a thought or event *cannot* result in an emotion of anger or fear. The best way to control the fight-or-flight response is by consciously controlling its polar opposite: the relax-and-release—or R & R— response.

HIDDEN POWERS OF THE BREATH

To the music world, R & R means rock and roll. To the army, it means rest and relaxation. To a cognitive scientist, a philosopher, or a spiritual seeker, it refers to the world's single most useful technique for turning attention to what really matters. The Christian tradition of contemplation as exemplified by the Benedictines, the Jewish kabbalistic tradition, and the Theravada Buddhist traditions all agree. For thousands of years, it's been well-known that focusing mental attention onto the breath is a great way to quiet the incessant chatter of the mind, allowing access to deeper spiritual levels. The folk remedy of taking a deep breath when you're angry derives from the same ancestral knowledge.

> THE SINGLE BEST WAY TO STIMULATE THE
> RELAX-AND-RELEASE RESPONSE, AND
> SHORT-CIRCUIT THE FIGHT-OR-FLIGHT RESPONSE, IS
> TO FOCUS YOUR MENTAL ATTENTION ONTO YOUR
> OWN BREATH. IT BUILDS MENTAL MUSCLE, TOO.

We'll discuss how breath work builds mental muscle. But first, do the following exercise.

The R & R Exercise

Again, instead of continuing to lecture on this subject, we'll ask you to commit to demonstrating for yourself how focus on the breath can stimulate the R & R response. Please take a minute and follow these directions as carefully as you can.

1. Please review the draw-a-breath chart and the breathing with the chart exercise in the introduction if you're not sure that you remember how to breathe along with this type of chart.

2. Now, as you did before, bring the image of your least favorite person (LFP) into your mind. Scan your body for tight shoulders, clenched teeth, shallow breath, or other symptoms of the anger or fear caused by the fight-or-flight response. If you are doing a good job of imagining your LFP, you should be experiencing some of these effects. Continue stewing over the image of your LFP for a few more seconds.

3. Quickly—keeping the LFP image in your mind—please turn to appendix A (page 136) and continue part 4 of the exercise without stopping.

BREATHING AND MENTAL MUSCLE

The neural path therapy method is structured somewhat like learning to play baseball. A beginning ballplayer first learns the most basic rules and strategies of the game. Simultaneously, he or she probably also begins two training programs. A specific skill-training program teaches the player to hit, throw, and catch a ball. A general exercise program builds strength, allowing the player to run faster, hit harder, and throw that ball with greater force. Similarly, in the neural path therapy method, while you learn the basics (about mental muscle, neural paths, the fight-or-flight and R & R responses), you will also follow two mental training programs. The first (which you'll work on now) is more general: a program to build mental muscle. The second is more specific: a program to create new, useful neural paths. You'll work on that in the next chapter (step two).

As we've said, mental muscle is what allows you to keep the power of your brain focused on an object or to move it to another object at will. This is easy to do with physical objects—for proof, just look up from these words to a clock or at your wristwatch. It's harder to do with mental objects (like thoughts or neural paths), perhaps because most of us have never been taught to do so.

Why Use the Breath to Build Mental Muscle?

In order to learn how to control your neural paths, you need to develop mental muscle—especially the kind used on mental, not physical, objects. Learning to focus your attention on the breathing process is a great way to do this. Why the breath? For one thing, it's always around (if it's not, you have more pressing problems than we can deal with in this book). In addition, the breath is so subtle, and so rarely observed, that it falls in between the category of physical objects and the category of mental objects. And, of course, it has the added advantage of stimulating the relax-and-release response.

Deep Focus

"I can focus fine, already." We sometimes hear people say this. "I go to the movies," they continue, "and stay focused on the new James Bond flick for two whole hours, with coming attractions." Or, "I get so involved in a good detective story, I don't even hear my kids fighting." Certainly, these examples demonstrate a form of focus. But they don't demonstrate mental muscle, because mental muscle is the ability to stay focused when there is no obvious reason to do so—no car chases, no scantily clad beautiful people, no clever and compelling story line and dialogue.

Imagine telling someone that you've been successfully training your dog to knock over trash cans to look for table scraps. Duuuh! Of course the dog is going to do that—it's the nature of a dog. And it's the nature of the brain to be attracted to exciting, or scary, or stimulating, or habitual thoughts, or neural paths. The real trick is to train your dog so that it will stay by your side, on command, when you need it there: when you're walking along a busy street and it sees a rival hound on the other side, or when you're passing your boss's house and the trash cans in front are loaded with juicy week-old leftovers.

Likewise, the crucial mental skill is to be able to focus attention onto—or away from—the thought, or neural path, of your choice. To turn your attention from a thought of your least favorite person to the breath. To keep your attention on work when thoughts of lunch or sex or basketball could so easily distract you.

To keep your attention on a beloved child or aged parent when thoughts of that risky big deal at work are so overwhelming (and tempting to indulge in). A well-trained dog is a joy to its master, while the poorly trained cur will bite the postman and make a mess on the carpet. A brain behaves similarly—it can be a joyous Aladdin's genie or the most hellish boss you've ever had. The difference lies in having mental muscle, and focus on the breath will help you to build it.

BATS, BIRDS, BEES, AND BARNACLES

The bat uses radar to interpret its world through its ears. A golden eagle is said to be able to see a rabbit from a mile away. A barnacle lacks both ears and eyes, but relates to its environment by combing the water around it with sensitive feeding and feeling appendages called "cirri." A bee interacts with the world around it by incessant kinetic (physical) activity.

Humans also have preferred ways of relating to their world, primarily through the senses: by hearing, by seeing, by feeling, by acting. There are also situations and times when one mode—visual, auditory, tactile, kinetic—may be more appropriate to use than another. So in the following pages, we will present mental muscle exercises based on seeing, hearing, feeling, and action. Try each one for a moment or two and see which you like best.

A Few Hints

Eventually, you'll be able to do these exercises—we hope— amidst noise and chaos, because that may be where you'll need them most. But to start with, give yourself a break. In your very first practice session (or the first few), make sure that you are in a quiet and comfortable spot where you won't be interrupted. Sit up straight. Don't slouch. (We're not sure why that helps, but it seems to.) Please don't get discouraged if you have trouble staying focused at first. We did too. So does everyone. And some of the exercises will be easier for you, others harder—but you won't know which ones they'll be until you've tried them all.

Warning: Two Neural Paths to Avoid

Even though you won't start working on identifying your own neural paths until chapter 2, there are two specific and counter-productive neural paths that you must learn to identify if you begin to feel like quitting this method. Should you find yourself traveling these—or similar—paths, *please commit to ignoring them for the next few days.* Just resolutely turn your attention back to the breathing exercise that has you perturbed, or, even better, try a different one.

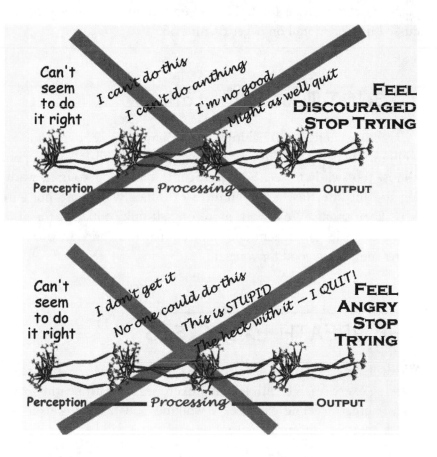

Self-Talk from Bad to Worse: Generalization and "Awfulizing"

Many of us have similar paths that are triggered when we realize that we can't easily learn something that we want to do. We then indulge in a type of processing called *self-talk*. This means exactly what it sounds like: you talk to yourself, going from one mental comment to another. Self-talk often tends to involve *generalization* ("This *always* happens to me!" or "She's *never* on time!") or *awfulizing* ("He probably won't call tonight. He probably won't call ever. No one will. I'll never have a date again in my whole life"). As a very broad generalization, men tend to be slightly more likely to follow the "this is stupid" self-talk path to anger, and women are slightly more likely to follow the "I'm no good" self-talk path to depression or angst. The anger and angst paths will be discussed in more detail on pages 65 and 66.

Self-Talk and Automaticity

As we mentioned, habitual paths may become, over time, so well-entrenched that the processing part—like self-talk—happens almost too swiftly to see. So once again, if you find yourself wanting to quit after just a few minutes of difficulty and are not sure why, keep trying. We'll work more on self-talk soon. But for now, please don't let an ancient and habitual pathway prevent you from doing something good for yourself.

THE BREATH EXERCISES

We will now present a series of breathing exercises: some breath drawing exercises, a breath labeling exercise, a breath hearing exercise, a breath feeling exercise, a walking and breathing exercise, and a breath counting exercise. Some of these will be more to your liking than others, depending on whether you're more like a bird, a bat, a bee, or a barnacle!

You've already learned how to breathe along with draw-a-breath charts. (At least we hope you have; if not, please go back to the introduction and practice.) Now it's time to start drawing your own breathing charts, instead of breathing along with our charts. If you are a visually oriented person—a bird, as it were—this will be a great exercise for you.

Prepare for these exercises by getting yourself some paper and a pen or pencil. Lined paper will be easier to use, at first. Just as you read from left to right with the draw-a-breath charts that you've already used, you'll be drawing from left to right to indicate the passage of time. A line moving upward indicates an inhale, a line moving down indicates an exhale, and a flat line indicates holding the breath. One line's worth of drawn breath might include anywhere from three to six slower breaths or a dozen faster ones. It's your breath and your chart, so draw it as you like. Three draw-a-breath exercises follow. The first will be easy, the second will be just a bit harder, and the third is more advanced (but still not too hard).

Breath Drawing Exercise: Slow and Steady

Start out by breathing—and simultaneously drawing—a reasonably slow and regular breath: no holds, nothing fancy. Just try to keep your pen or pencil moving as you breath, angling up as you inhale, and down as you exhale. Your chart might look like the following one if you breathed (and drew) four nice, slow, even breaths, starting with your lungs empty (on an inhale, that is). The fourth breath, at right, is a bit shallower and sharper (changing more crisply from inhale to exhale) than the first three. Please remember: This chart is just an example. Rather than breathing along with our chart, the point of this exercise lies in drawing your own chart *while* you breathe.

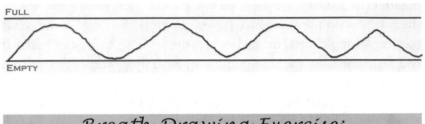

Breath Drawing Exercise: Fast and Slow

Now chart your own breath as you breathe less evenly or regularly: go slower or faster, deeper or shallower. Just try to observe how you are breathing and represent it graphically. The breath should come first: in other words, *do not* try to breathe what you are drawing; instead, try to draw what you are breathing! Of course, that's harder to do when you are consciously trying to make your breath more varied, as in this exercise. Here's what your chart might look like if you started with a slow, even breath, followed by three fast, sharp breaths, then a very slow breath with a deep exhale (so deep that it goes *under* the "lungs comfortably empty" line).

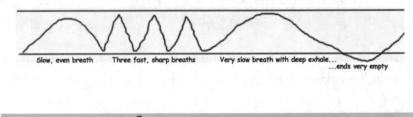

Slow, even breath   Three fast, sharp breaths   Very slow breath with deep exhale...
...ends very empty

Breath Drawing Exercise: Getting Fancy with Holds

Please spend some time drawing simple breaths—just using in and out lines—before adding some hold lines, as in the fancy chart that follows. It represents four breaths, three of them quite odd (so we've written out the ins, outs, and holds for you). The first breath starts with three sharp little inhales, each followed by a brief hold: in! in! in! This first breath ends with a more normal exhale. The second breath starts normally, with a long inhale and a short hold before the exhale. But the exhale is composed of three little out-puffs of air, each with a short hold: out! out! out! followed by a slower out. The third breath is a nice, even, slow one. The fourth starts with a sharp inhale and a short hold. The exhale is like a sigh—a fast, partial exhale that fades into a slower, deep exhale.

You may find it easier to begin this exercise by breathing along with our chart below. This will help you get used to drawing the holds (which most of us don't even notice at all as we breathe). After you've breathed along with this chart a few times, get out your scrap paper and chart your own breath, making sure to include some holds.

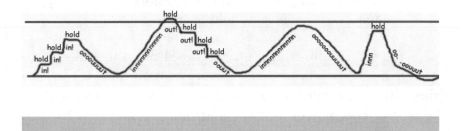

Drawing Without Controlling

Once you get the hang of breath drawing, it will be easier to just follow your breath without trying to control it in any way. If you like, you can always set some time aside for "Oh wow! I'll do a really long inhale then ten little out puffs; it'll look so cool." But that's just technical practice for the drawing part and not the real point of the exercise, which is using the charting process to pay incredibly close attention to each and every breath.

Draw-a-breath exercises are perfect for using anytime you have a pen or pencil and a scrap of paper handy. Try this during a

boring meeting (one where you don't have to pay too much attention to the speaker) or while you're on hold during a phone call.

The Breath Labeling Exercise

This exercise often appeals to the bats among us—those for whom
hearing is a favorite sense. It is very simple to learn, although it's not
always easy to stay focused on for long. Just observe the inhale, the
exhale, and (if there is one) the hold part of your breath. Whisper
"innnnn" silently to yourself as long as you are inhaling. Whisper
"hold" if you are holding. Whisper "ooouuuut" if you are exhaling.
Listen to yourself as you do the exercise:

> "innnnnn … hold … oooouuuuut … innn … oouut …
> innnnnn … oooouuuut … hold … innn … ooout…"

You can do this with your eyes closed or open, although it's
good to practice all these exercises with eyes open (in case you need
them while you're running away from something). Don't try to regu-
larize your breathing in any way. Just observe and label; let each
breath be different—longer, shorter, deeper, shallower—if it wants
to be.

Use this exercise anywhere and anytime. One of the beauties
of this exercise is that no one can tell when you're practicing. Get
in the habit of doing it for only one or two breaths at a time. Learn
to leap into this exercise while you have even a few free seconds of
mental space in the middle of a task. Then return to your task a
bit more relaxed and refreshed. We like to do this one as soon as
we hear the phone ring—there's plenty of time to label a single
normal-speed breath and pick up before the third ring.

Breath Hearing Exercise

If you'd like some extra sound input—and are in a place where you can do it discreetly—use this variation on the previous exercise. Breathe through your mouth with your lips only slightly open. You'll get a very quiet whistling sound on the inhale. As you exhale, whisper a long "aaaaaaah" for the entire length of the exhale. Focus your mental attention onto the actual sound of your breath rather than on mentally saying the "innnnnn" or "hoooold" or "ooouuut" as you've done before.

Feeling the Breath

The barnacles among us may prefer to focus attention on the breath through the sense of touch, or feeling. To do this, breathe in through your mouth and out through your nose. As you inhale, focus your attention on the sensation of coolness as the air hits the inside of your mouth (this may be easier to do if your mouth is only slightly open, so that the breath accelerates as it passes through your lips). When you exhale, focus your attention on the sensation of the air passing out through your nostrils. As with all the breathing exercises, the key is to stay as focused as possible on the breath and the sensation that it produces. If any other thought enters your mind, try to notice that your attention has lapsed and bring your focus back to the breath. That's what builds your mental muscle!

This is another exercise that you can do anywhere, anytime, for as long or short as you like or have time for—even for a single breath or two. You can experiment by combining this with the breath labeling exercise to stimulate your senses of touch and hearing simultaneously.

Walking and Breathing Exercise

Perhaps, like a bee, you prefer to relate to the world in an active, rather than a visual, auditory, or feel-based, way. If you are an athletic or even a "jumpy" person who "just can't sit still," you may fall into this category. If you do, this exercise may suit you better than the draw-a-breath, breath labeling, or breath feeling exercises, and it may be easier to fit into your lifestyle.

In this exercise, you are simply trying to keep your attention focused well enough on your breathing and your walking so that you can tell how many steps you take during each inhale and each exhale. Every time your foot touches the ground counts as a step. Start with your lungs comfortably empty, and begin your inhale as a foot hits the ground, counting silently "in." Continue to inhale and count: the next footfall is "two," the one after that "three" and so on. When you want to exhale, try to change to the exhale exactly as your foot hits the floor, counting that first step as "out." The next footfall is "two," and so on. You are *not* going to draw a chart for this exercise, but we've provided one to illustrate how the breath and the steps relate. This chart covers a time period that includes a full in-breath, the subsequent out-breath, and a small portion of the next in-breath. As you can see, the walker takes four steps during the inhale and four steps during the exhale.

As you do this exercise, you'll probably find that you don't take the same number of steps during the inhale as during the exhale. And your step count will most likely vary from breath to breath, although joggers may fall into a very consistent rhythm.

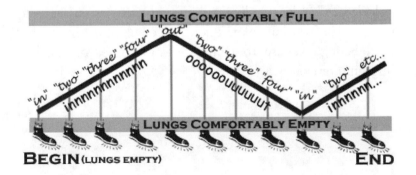

You can do this exercise anywhere and anytime you're walking. Choose a short, repetitive walking task (such as "every time I use the stairs to my apartment" or "every time I walk from my desk to the printer") and commit to doing this exercise during that walk—every time you take it. Even a single breath's worth will be valuable if you do it often enough, since all these breathing exercises have a cumulative effect on your mental muscle. If you are a hiker or a jogger, try it in the mountains or during a run.

Breath Counting Exercise

Here's another breathing exercise that's easy to do anywhere, anytime—without anyone noticing. Forget about bats or birds or other animals; this exercise tends to appeal to a mix of people who use their minds a lot: those who are orderly, those who like math, analytical types, and, conversely, those who have a tendency for disorganized or rapid thought patterns. To do it, you'll simply count each breath as described below.

Start at the beginning of an inhale by mentally labeling it as "in one." As soon as you begin the first exhale, label it "out one." As soon as you start the second inhale, label it "in two." As soon as you begin the second exhale, label it "out two." To start with, just count four breaths at a time. That seems like a good, manageable number for most people.

"in one ... out one ...... in two ... out two ...... in three ... out three ...... in four ... out four ..."

When you've finished your fourth breath, start over at "in one...out one."

Again, do it anywhere, anytime. Since counting (at least up to four) is a skill learned very young and practiced often, some people find this an easy exercise to do in noisy or even distracting situations.

The Mini Exercise Regime

These are just very short mental muscle exercises that you throw in during the day, even for as little as a single breath or two. Choose one or more of the breathing exercises—drawing, labeling, hearing, feeling, walking, or counting—that you just learned and think of ways you can fit them into your daily schedule at work, at home, or in between.

Commit to doing these "minis" for a total of at least five minutes a day, even if that total is made up of a few dozen exercises, a single breath at a time. Some people find that putting a sticky note—saying something like *Breathe!* or *Focus!*—on the computer or refrigerator helps to remind them to do their minis!

Which Way Is Best?

It doesn't really matter which exercise or exercises you choose to do—the results are the same. Your trigger thought is the decision to do a breathing exercise. The process involves refocusing your mental attention onto the breath. It doesn't matter why you decided to refocus. It doesn't matter what style of breathing exercise you use. The end result—if you do the exercise to the best of your ability—will be an alert but relaxed state of mind.

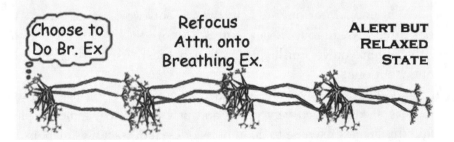

Breathing Exercise Review

1. Please try all of the above exercises for at least a minute or so each.

2. Choose one or more that you like.

3. Decide when you'll have opportunities to do it (or them) during the day.

4. Commit yourself to doing it (or them) as often as possible, even for the very short time periods that we call "minis." Doing an exercise for half a minute ten times a day will be far more beneficial than *attempting* (but failing) to make time to do it once a day for half an hour.

REAL-LIFE USE

Imagine a weight-lifting coach. What would be his or her first and most important piece of advice? Don't start with a 300-pound weight! The best way to demoralize or even injure beginning weight lifters is to make them try to use a weight that's too heavy. Instead, a good trainer will have the student use a light weight until he or she has learned the motions and balance skills needed to do the lift, whether curl or press or squat. Then—and only then—is it time to up the ante and add a few five- pound plates to the bar.

Of course, it's easy to understand the progressive nature of a physical endeavor such as weight lifting. And no one would judge harshly a brand new, white-belt karate student who didn't want to try out her self-defense moves against a bar full of mean drunks. Yet sadly, some of us would judge ourselves harshly for trying—and failing—to use the dictates of a self-help book on our most long-term and deep-seated problems.

Certainly, most people who would buy a book of this type have real issues and problems that they want to deal with. That's probably why you're reading these words right now. Perhaps you're even in a crisis or near-crisis situation. So it's a painful paradox that, in order to deal with your problem or crisis, you must first learn new skills that may not seem to be of instantaneous use. But like the neophyte weight lifter or novice martial artist, you'll need to apply your breath focus skills in a progressive way, starting with a mild real-life annoyance rather than your deepest fear or most infuriating anger.

Practicing What You Preach

Unless you plan to live in a Buddhist monastery or take vows with the Benedictines, the entire purpose of the neural path therapy method is to use the material in real-life situations. But since you don't want to start lifting with a 300-pound weight, it's time to choose a mildly annoying situation in which to apply your breath-focus skills.

The Waiting-on-Line Exercise: Preparation

Here's a brief step-by-step description of the process that you'll use to prepare yourself for a real-life use of what you've learned so far. We'll discuss each of these elements in detail in the next pages.

1. Choose a particular, specific scenario in which you're prone to get mildly annoyed.

2. Make a commitment to using any one of your breathing exercises (or a combination) during that situation.

3. Visualize the situation, as described in the next section.

4. Once you are visualizing the stressful situation, begin to do an *actual* breathing exercise as part of your visualization.

5. During your visualization, play with the point of no return (PONR), which we'll discuss in a moment.

6. Repeat the last three steps a few times.

CHOOSING THE SCENARIO

What's a good place to start using your new skills? Well, a mildly annoying situation fits the bill for a number of reasons. Mild annoyance, by definition, is a low-stakes emotion. No one will get hurt if you can't stay focused on the breathing exercise. Also, annoyance, which is a weak form of anger, is physically easy to identify as resulting from the fight part of the fight-or-flight response. It's also very satisfying to be able to overcome even a mild annoyance that has peeved you for decades.

For many people, waiting on line at the bank, the grocery store, the pharmacy, or elsewhere during lunch hour provides an appropriate real-life challenge. Since your time is limited (and of course, the line will take longer than you want it to), this situation is slightly stressful, and it happens regularly (so you won't have to wait years to put the material in this book into practice). A segment of traffic-ridden commute (but not with you as the driver, yet) may also be an appropriate starting place. Or try it in a low-stakes interaction with an annoying colleague. No matter the scenario, the process is the same. So let's consider the act of waiting on line as an example.

THE COMMITMENT

It's part of the deal—you have to make an agreement with yourself that you're going to make a good-faith effort in the chosen scenario. It may not be easy. You may have excellent excuses (your foot hurts, or there's only one register open, or the person in front of you has six badly behaved children). But once you decide in advance on the time and place to try this, you're committed. Since you'll have invested time and energy in this project long before you set foot on that line—by practicing the visualization exercise that follows—it will be easy to maintain your commitment.

CHOOSING THE BREATH-FOCUS EXERCISE

You may choose (and commit to using) a specific single breath-focus exercise for your real-life experiment and for the visualization practice sessions which precede it. Or you may want to keep your options open and simply commit to using any of the breath exercises or any combination of them. Single exercise or a combination, it's up to you; choose whichever seems more likely to work.

USE YOUR IMAGINATION AND ALL YOUR SENSES

Once you've chosen your scenario and committed yourself to using a breathing exercise on it, try to visualize the situation using as many of your senses as you can. Here's an example of how you might create a multisensory visualization, using a visit to the supermarket as an example.

A VISUALIZED VISIT TO THE SUPERMARKET

As you approach the checkout area, your hands feel the slightly slimy plastic of the shopping cart's handle. You peruse the checkout lanes that divide the crowd into inscrutable columns of humanity, one line per cash register. Which will be fastest? Impossible to tell. You can smell the sweat of your fellow customers, hear the Muzak—faux Beatles. You can see Cashier #1 yakking to her girlfriend the bagger while carefully avoiding the irate glances of the customers in her line. Cashier #2 is witlessly perusing another customer's problematic debit card, clueless. Cashier #3 seems alert and on the ball, but her customer is irate and more interested in complaining about the state of the vegetable aisle than in finishing his transaction. All the while, you wait, as the clock ticks and your lunch hour grows shorter and shorter. You're starting to get stressed out, naturally. It's a familiar, if not a pleasant, neural path that you've trod many times.

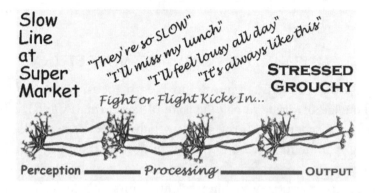

VISUALIZE AND DO A BREATH EXERCISE

However, instead of engaging in unpleasant self-talk ("That cashier's an idiot! I'll never have time to eat. I'll probably feel lousy all afternoon, from hunger …"), visualize yourself successfully focusing all of your attention on counting (or labeling) each breath.

Here's the critical component: as you do this part of the visualization (*imagining* yourself effortlessly doing your chosen breath exercise, or combination of breath exercises, during the stressful scenario), you'll be practicing an *actual* breathing exercise.

This blurs the line between visualization and real-life use of the exercise (since you're really doing the breathing exercise while you visualize) and will make the real-life usage easier (and more likely to be successful). What's really happening, of course, is that you are creating a new neural path, simply by rehearsing it in your mind. We'll talk about the implications of this type of rehearsal later, but for now … just do it!

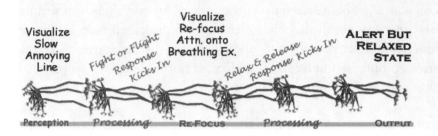

PLAYING THE POINT OF NO RETURN

During your visualization and breath focus, practice playing on the edge of what we call *the point of no return* (PONR). This is the exact moment when the fight-or-flight response really kicks in, making it difficult to return your attention to the breathing exercise. Even in an artificial situation like a visualization, you can notice this point approaching *before* it hits the fan—if you pay attention to two things: self-talk and fight-or-flight response symptoms.

Here's what will happen. During the visualization and breathing exercise, your attention wanders away from the breath, and you indulge in some self-talk: "How can Cashier #1 be so lazy, Cashier #2 so dumb, and the customer at Cashier #3 so inconsiderate? This shouldn't happening to me. I'm going to miss lunch." You feel your fight-or-flight response start to kick in. But you notice this happening, and you simply return your attention to your breathing: "innnnnn, oooouuuut…innnn, ooouuut…"

EMOTIONAL HIJACKING

If you are expecting it to occur, you have a better chance of not getting hijacked by an emotional response. As soon as you feel your attention deviating from the breathing exercise, see if you are indeed talking to yourself. Sometimes just noticing what you are doing makes it easier to stop. Also, try to be aware of the tightening of your shoulders, or jaw, or hands, or any other symptom of the fight-or-flight response. If you feel them, try to consciously relax the tight spots, and redouble your efforts to stay focused on the breathing. Sometimes, switching to a new breathing exercise helps—from breath labeling to breath counting, for instance. The change is interesting enough to engage your brain for the extra few seconds that make the difference. That's why choosing a single exercise to stick to may be less effective than planning on using a combination of exercises.

PRACTICE MAKES MORE PERFECT

Practice the above steps—visualize, do the breath focus, and play with the PONR—at least a few times. Each practice session should only take a minute or two to visualize the scenario, a minute or less to get into the breathing exercise, then a minute or so to play with the point of no return. After a few of these, you'll have created a robust new neural path that you're ready to try out in real life.

Now Go for It, in Real Time

Now it's time to hit the busy supermarket during lunch; hop on the bus during rush hour; sit next to that annoying colleague during your coffee break. Try to put the new neural path that you've practiced—in which an annoying scenario doesn't trigger a fight-or-flight response but instead tells you to focus on a breathing exercise—into real-life action. Good luck!

WHAT HAPPENED?

You tried the real-life application of the new neural path. Now it's time to evaluate the results. There are three potential outcomes: it was easy to use the new path, you couldn't apply the new path at all, or—most likely—you had some degree of success, however limited, in using it. Let's consider each of these outcomes.

If the Real-Life Experiment Was Somewhat Successful...

If you were somewhat successful, you probably were able to refocus your attention onto the breath at least part of the time, even if doing so was difficult. You are now ready to start looking for additional, similar opportunities to practice on. In other words, look for other scenarios that tend to trigger a neural path that leads to a negative emotion. Then apply the six-part preparation process (page 41) to each new annoying situation. It may be useful, once you are trying to use a breath focus exercise on a few of these situations, to make a mental or physical list of them; for example:

1. Stand in bank line.

2. Give dog a bath.

3. Pay phone bill online.

4. Have dinner with spouse's ex.

Having a list will help you remember your commitment to working with them. You should also continue to practice doing mental muscle exercises *without* real-life use. Make it easy to fit these into your daily life, using the mini exercise regime that we described earlier in this chapter.

If the Real-Life Experiment Was Easy...

By "easy," we mean that you were able to stay mostly focused on the breathing exercise, and that doing this made the mildly annoying situation, well, not pleasant, but at least time not wasted (since you put in a few moments on building mental muscle during it). If this was the case for you, look for additional opportunities to apply the breath-focus skills. You can choose somewhat more diffi-cult scenarios to practice with, but don't start lifting 300-pound weights yet. Work your way up gradually! You may want to come up with a list (see previous section) to help remind you of the sce-narios that you want to work on.

If the Real-Life Experiment Was Really Hard...

By "hard," we mean that you were not able to shift your attention from the annoying situation to the breathing exercise. This should come as no surprise. After having spent your entire adult life thus far feeling annoyed when you end up on the slowest line at the supermarket, it's not unlikely that your first attempt at creating a new neural path for that encounter was not so success-ful. Instead of spending those fifteen minutes in blissful contempla-tion of your breath, you may have seesawed between annoyance and breath focus (with emphasis on the former). That's natural. If this was the case for you, we have some suggestions.

Keep Building More Mental Muscle

Continue to work with the breathing exercises by them-selves—that is, *not* in real-life situations. Please go back to either the most basic draw-a-breath exercise on page 8 (Breathing with the Chart), the R & R exercise on page 25, or the slightly more varied exercises on pages 32 to 38. This will help you identify and build mental muscle.

Put in a total of at least thirty or forty minutes of mini exer-cises (*not* one long chunk) at the mental gym.

Try Again, but Choose an Easier Scenario

Our second suggestion? Try another real-life experiment. This time, choose a mildly annoying situation that is even milder—if your last experience was difficult and frustrating, you probably chose too heavy a weight to start lifting. Also, pick a situation of very short duration; it's easier to refocus attention onto the breath—and keep it there—during a thirty-second encounter with a surly colleague than during a long wait on a slow line!

What If It's Still Difficult?

If you tried working with even milder annoyances, but you still had trouble with the real-life application of the breathing exercises, here are three important suggestions.

Warning: Self-Sabotage Path Ahead!

If you are having trouble with the real-life application, it would be easy to allow yourself to fall into one of the two unuseful neural paths ("I'm no good; I'll just quit" or "This is stupid. I quit"). Please don't.

Keep on Reading

If necessary, forget about the real-life exercise for a while, and just keep reading this book as you work on your mental muscle building. Later steps will help you to return to the real-life exercise and achieve success with it.

If you like, as you continue reading the book, every so often choose a progressively easier (less annoying) real-life situation to try your breath-focus skills on. Soon you'll start seeing results, and you can return to the harder ones!

Lemons to Lemonade: Using the PONR

Okay. You keep getting grumpy in the checkout lane. But the real-life experiment is only a failure if you fail to use the crucially important information that it can provide. Use your less than fully successful experience as an opportunity to learn more about the situation itself and about your personal PONR. So if you blow it and get annoyed, don't get mad—just consider it as part of the experiment, for research purposes. Here are some useful inquiries to make:

1. What exactly makes you lose the breath focus and return to your typical response?

2. Is it due to an external event (noise, long wait, hunger, heat or cold, rude cashier) or a mental event (self-talk, a particular thought, unnoticed attack of the fight-or-flight response)?

3. Can you feel your point of no return approaching? Or did it sneak up on you? Were there any hints, in retrospect, that it was coming?

4. Are you aware of any self-talk? Any symptoms of the fight-or-flight response? Tight shoulders? Clenched teeth?

Why This Is So Important

It may seem silly to concern yourself to this extent with such an inconsequential event—especially one that seems difficult and frustrating, and which you'd like to forget about entirely. But the same elements that cause you to lose your cool on the checkout line will have a similar effect on any situation that you need to cope with. So this is really important work—please take a deep breath, be patient, and continue.

The Point of No Return (PONR) Scan Exercise

Here's one more exercise that's useful for everyone, even though it may not be the most pleasant one that we'll give you. Learning to identify the symptoms of your point of no return, and practicing the breath focus to defuse it, is a tremendous help in short-circuiting a fight-or-flight response. The sooner you can identify the fight-or-flight response, the sooner you can stimulate the relax-and-release response to counter it.

1. Visualize one of your troublesome scenarios (the boss just lit a big cigar in that little office) or a thought that's apt to provoke an emotional response (new engine at only 58,000 miles? Grr!).

2. While you do this, scan your entire body for signs of an approaching fight-or-flight response: hot cheeks? tingling scalp? clenched teeth? butterflies in your stomach? Try to notice the symptoms in their earliest, most subtle, stages.

3. Then turn your mind to your breath, killing two birds with one stone (identifying PONR symptoms and building mental muscle).

4. This should defuse the fight-or-flight response and reverse the symptom, or symptoms.

You'll find that similar emotional reactions will tend to have similar symptoms. That is, if one angry thought produces clenched teeth, most of your angry thoughts will. But your fear thoughts—all of them, no matter the cause—may tend to produce butterflies in the stomach.

Summing Up

No matter the level of success (or lack thereof) you may have experienced in your first or subsequent real-life neural path therapy adventures, please go on to step two. There, you'll practice learning to notice and analyze your own neural paths, which will help you to use step one—the power of the breath and the mental muscle that it builds—to control those paths more skillfully.

CHAPTER 2

Step Two

Thought Watching: Your Neural Neighborhood

In step one, you practiced using the power of the breath to activate the R & R response by

- Taking your attention away from thoughts that stimulate the fight-or-flight response

- Putting your attention onto the breath (thus stimulating the relax-and-release response)

You may have used our waiting-on-line suggestion, the unpleasant commute, or the annoying coworker for your real-life experiment. But it doesn't really matter which problematic situation you chose to work with. Nor does it matter how successful your experiment was. Whether you experienced half an hour of blissful mental muscle building or thirty minutes of annoyance and self-criticism, it's time for step two.

WHAT'S NEW IN STEP TWO

However your real-life experience in step one turned out, in step two you'll continue to explore both the neural path therapy method, and the contents of your own mind. The first part of step two will help you to

- Understand the nature and impact of thoughts on your life

- Identify the most common types of neural paths, including unnecessary fears, inappropriate desires, interpersonal aggravations, anger, and angst

In the second part of step two, you'll learn to

- Watch your own thoughts, just as you watch objects in the real world

- Pinpoint the troublesome or unuseful paths in your own "neural neighborhood"

- Use the dead-end technique to create new and more skillful paths to replace them with

Please don't forget to continue your work on real-life experiments as described at the end of step one while you concentrate on the new material in step two.

THE NATURE AND IMPACT OF THOUGHTS

Although not real in a physical sense, we all know that thoughts can have a profound effect, positive or negative, on every aspect of human life. A fear thought could save your life by discouraging you from pursuing an attractive but risky course of action. An anger thought, inappropriately acted on, could ruin it ("I didn't mean to punch the police officer, your honor; I just saw red for a minute").

The Bad News: Stress Unlimited

The physical effect of thoughts on the body can also be both bad and good. In the least favorite person exercise, you saw that a thought can trigger a fight-or-flight response and produce an emotion, flooding your body with hormones, electrical impulses, and chemicals. Do a good, sincere job of imagining someone that you loathe with a passion, and your body will react almost as though this person were actually present. So you've already demonstrated for yourself that, on certain levels, the body reacts to a thought of a physical object (your LFP) similarly to how it reacts to a physical object (the LFP in the flesh). Imagine your boss approaching with pink slip in hand—ten times a day—and you daily add ten good-sized doses of stress to your life, even though you may never get canned in real life.

The Good News: Visualization Works

On the plus side, repeatedly rehearsing an event in the mind (as you did with the visualizations in the real-life experiment of step one) helps to create an actual neural path, almost as though you were repeatedly performing the event in real life. Practice something in the mind, and if you can visualize it clearly enough, it becomes easier to do in real life. From Olympic athletes to top sales personnel, many people use visualization to enhance performance, simply because it works.

On a More Subtle Level ...

Just as important, yet even harder to notice, is the fact that people often confuse thoughts with reality. Please demonstrate this for yourself in the following exercise.

The Thought Versus Reality (TVSR) Exercise

Get ready, please, to breathe along with another draw-a-breath chart, as closely as you can. Just turn to appendix B, and—as soon as you get there—start following the chart with your breath. Ready? Get set. Go!

WHY NEURAL PATH MAPPING IS IMPORTANT

Neural path mapping offers a convenient visual way to conceptualize thought processes in the brain—the same mental processes that produce your emotions and actions. This is important for two reasons.

- Learning to see neural paths as mental objects—as things that you can change and manipulate, rather than as built-in reactions that are as immutable as your height—allows you to control them, rather than the other way around.

- Learning to identify the specific paths that produce painful emotions or unuseful deeds in your life, *before* they go into action, makes it easier to replace them with more skillful paths.

That's why you need to get the hang of mapping out your own particular neural neighborhood—so that you can navigate it with greater ease and finesse.

Parts of the Neural Path

Let's review the elements of a neural path.

- You *perceive* a physical event or a mental event (a thought).

- This perception triggers a *process* (which could be a hardwired response or a series of thoughts, including self-talk thoughts).

- This process results in an *output*, which might be an emotion or an action.

As you may remember, a hardwired response is an automatic response that you are born with, like a fear response if you find yourself falling. And you can also create your own automatic responses just by using a particular path so often that you no longer even notice the processing part, since you no longer have to think about it, and it happens too swiftly to see. Here's a diagram summing up what we've just discussed.

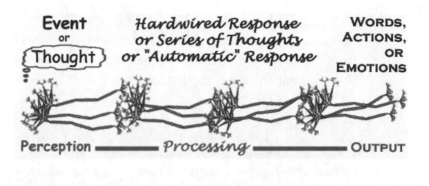

Draw-It-Yourself Neural Path

It's easy to create your own neural path diagrams. Please try to draw a diagram of a thought-triggered neural path right now. Think of perception to processing to output as a general recipe, and plug in your own ingredients:

1. Start with writing down the thought that triggers the path.

2. Add any self-talk or linked thought process that triggers the fight-or-flight response (if this is a path that has been made automatic by long use, just write "automatic" above the processing part, unless you can tease out the thoughts that occur too swiftly to see).

3. Lastly, note the emotional state that you end up in.

Fill in the blanks on the next page, or draw your own from scratch, and don't bother to draw the neurons unless you want to!

Now would be an excellent time to draw a few more neural paths. It may seem silly (especially if you are not a visually oriented person). But drawing neural paths is a great way to show them as the objects—if mental objects—that they are.

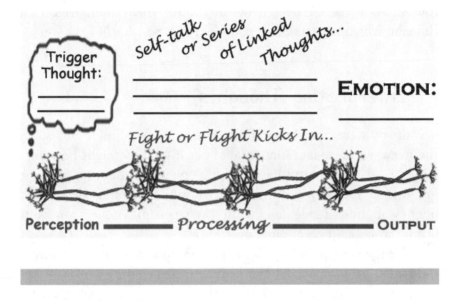

WHY THOUGHT WATCHING IS IMPORTANT

Before we continue, there's one more thing you must understand: often an event triggers a thought, and it is this thought—not the event itself—that then triggers the processing part of the neural path. Here's a diagram showing this type of path:

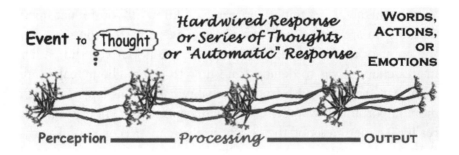

This diagram and the similar-looking one at the top of page 59 may look alike, but the diagram on the top of page 59 shows a path triggered by an event *or* a thought. The diagram on the bottom shows a path triggered by an event, which then triggers a thought, which triggers the rest of the path. So what?

Interpreting Thoughts

If you were from Mars, driving with an Earthling friend down the freeway at a sedate ninety miles per hour, you might be entertained to see the pretty flashing blue and red lights atop the car just behind you. If you were the Earthling, desperately dependent upon your automobile, and with two speeding tickets on your license, you might react quite differently.

Or say your friend and you see a mutual acquaintance across the street. You wave, but the acquaintance ignores you. You are insulted and angry, and your emotions may affect your future actions ("Why, Jones just blew me off. What a jerk. Forget about helping move his stupid couch tomorrow!"), but your friend reacts differently—he already knows that the acquaintance lost both contact lenses this morning and can't see you. In each case, the interpretation of the event—that is, the thought about the event, not the event itself—is what triggered an emotional response.

More Confusion

In the above examples, at least you know (if you reflect upon it) that you are responding to a physical event with a thought. But the point of the TVSR experiment that (we hope) you did earlier in this chapter was to demonstrate how thoughts about reality are often hard to distinguish from the reality itself. This makes it even more important to watch your thoughts with care. Thoughts about reality—sometimes not the reality itself—can trigger neural paths that may have profound or even lifelong effects. Consider some of the most important categories of thoughts and paths, like the ones that form your beliefs and biases, your fears and desires, or the ones that affect your interpersonal relationships.

BEYOND ANNOYANCE

Up until now, most of your work has been with paths built from a mild form of the fight part of the fight-or-flight response—that is, paths involving annoying situations (the supermarket wait, the unpleasant commute, the annoying colleague). It's time to investigate other types of emotions. In the following section, we'll consider beliefs and biases, fear (which comes from the flight part of the fight-or-flight response), desire (another ancient and often hardwired one), and interpersonal emotion, and end with a discussion of anger (the extreme version of annoyance) and angst (that Germanic combination of all things painful and negative). At the end of this chapter, after introducing the dead-end strategy, we'll provide some preparatory exercises for beginning to work with these emotions.

Beliefs

You can believe in many things: a philosophy, a leader, a religion. But the most important kind of belief, in our definition, is simply a long-term and deeply held thought about yourself—in other words, a thought that has become automatic, not to be investigated or questioned. A thought of this type becomes part of your self-image, that is, how you see yourself in your mind's eye.

Beliefs are often formed when we are young. They may be a result of external events—if you tried to play sports many times as a child without much success, you may have formed the belief "I am unathletic." If you were often told "You're stupid," or "A real man never admits that he's wrong," after a while, you may have started to believe it.

Obviously, a belief may be true, or it may be false. Unfortunately, most beliefs about the self have become so automatic that you never question them.

Biases

A bias is a deeply held thought about others (who are often considered as a group rather than as individuals) that is automatic, unquestioned. "Harmonica players are egotists." "Men are such pigs." "People from the XYZ group are all idiots."

Like beliefs, biases may have elements of truth. Unlike beliefs, they are virtually never entirely true or false, since individuals within any group will vary. But if biases are automatic—beneath the level of conscious observation—how can you test them against the reality of any given individual?

Old Habits Die Hard

Many beliefs and biases are developed at an early age—especially beliefs about yourself. Left unexplored, they are like lurking time bombs, sabotaging you from the past.

MANY OF OUR NEURAL PATHS WERE DEVELOPED AT AN EARLY AGE.

WE HAVE TRAVELED THEM SO OFTEN THAT THE PROCESSING PART HAS BECOME AUTOMATIC, AND DIFFICULT TO SEE CONSCIOUSLY.

WHEN WE FOLLOW AN OLD PATH, WE ARE BRINGING THE PAST INTO OUR PRESENT.

THIS AFFECTS OUR FUTURE.

Fears and Phobias

If anger is the fight half of the fight-or-flight response, fear represents our modern version of the flight part. Like desire, fear goes way back. Originally developed in early forms of life to help organisms avoid danger and pain, it has many positive uses today—if our fears represent a realistic appraisal of reality. Fear can save us from engaging in dangerous behavior ("I'm scared to climb that rusty old water tower while I'm drunk") and act as a motivator ("If I don't finish this project, I'll lose my job").

Unfortunately, many of us suffer from repetitive fear thoughts that may or may not be realistic (like the example of the boss with pink slip). Realistic or not, if repeated fear thoughts are used neither to help us avoid danger nor to motivate positive behavior, they only add extra stress to lives that have plenty already.

Fear is an emotion, the output of a neural path in which an event or thought (or event, then thought) triggers the flight part of the fight-or-flight response. This path naturally has a profound effect on the body, as is clear from the abundance of slang that describes it: the heart rate goes up ("chickenhearted"), the stomach tightens ("butterflies in the stomach"), the muscles may fail to work ("weak-kneed"), the extremities shake ("the jitters").

When fear goes beyond the body and affects behavior, it produces a phobia. You may be fearful of flying, but if you still fly when you really need to, you are simply the victim of fear. When your fear prevents you from flying for an important trip, you are the victim of a phobia. Later, we'll introduce an exercise that will help you to begin coping with your less overwhelming fears. With practice, you'll be able to apply the same techniques to more intimidating ones.

Needs and Greeds: On Desire

Pope Gregory the Great, in the late sixth century, was almost certainly not thinking of neural paths when he created his list of the Seven Deadly Sins. However, it's worth pointing out that even way back then, five of the seven worst things a person could do (in Gregory's opinion, at least) were avarice, gluttony, lust, envy, and pride—all related to issues of desire, appetite, or craving.

Desire is old—very old. Since the first virus replicated itself (the ancestor of the sex act), since the first amoeba engulfed a piece of food, desire has been part of life, and many needs are hardwired into the modern human brain. If all we needed was a bit of food, some water, and enough air to breath, life would be simple for most of us. Unfortunately, many greeds—unnecessary or extravagant desires—are built upon that ancient hardwiring.

Learning to differentiate between need and greed, then learning to determine what is realistic or achievable to want, is difficult in our material-based culture. It's also difficult to control desires that are just slightly perverted versions of natural needs, like those involving eating (or overeating) and sex. We'll explore these issues with an exercise toward the end of step two, and the information and exercises of steps three and four may also help you to deal more skillfully with this ancient issue.

Interpersonal Applications

Hermits and castaways on desert islands don't have to worry about interpersonal relationships. Most of the rest of us do, whether with parents or children, friends or lovers or spouses, colleagues or bosses or subordinates. The issues described above—beliefs, biases, fears, and desires—plus the annoyance that we dealt with in step one, can all enter into our interactions with others. And there's one more, which you may not be familiar with, unless you're in the psychology trade.

Transference

Transference is a subcategory of the TVSR problem, as demonstrated in the exercise on page 56. In this exercise, you saw how easy it is to confuse your thoughts about reality with the reality itself—sometimes not seeing the real Mary, your low-maintenance friend, but instead, looking at your mental image, your thought, of Mary. In transference, you look at person A but are seeing your thought of person B.

For example, your boss may remind you, consciously or not, of your father. If this is the case, and especially if this occurs below the level of conscious thought, you may react to him as though you were reacting to your father. Perhaps you experience a greater need to attain his approval, perhaps a greater need to rebel—that would depend on how you related to dear old Dad. Being on the lookout for transference issues is a good idea when you find a relationship of any kind to be problematic, or when a relationship seems to be more stressful than you would expect it to be. Transference is often an issue between couples, since people often tend to continue working out issues that began with their parents, using lovers as convenient, if unwitting, substitutes!

Two Biggies: Angst and Anger

Two of the most common and most general neural path categories—angst and anger—represent strategies for dealing with the world. First mentioned on page 29, these two troublesome paths are often based on long-term, habitual self-talk—how you explain the world and its frustrations to yourself.

Anger 101

If your tendency when hurt or frustrated is to attribute blame to others or the world ("He shouldn't do that to me!" or "It shouldn't be that way!"), then you take the way of anger. Can't focus on the breath? "This is stupid. I quit!"

You've already worked with annoyance in step one. Since both annoyance and anger are emotions produced by the fight part of the fight-or-flight response, the difference between them is mainly one of intensity. It's also one of speed, since anger often has an exaggerated automaticity—you "fly into a rage," as the saying goes (hardly anyone saunters or strolls into a rage). Strong feelings of anger are very hard to work with. Please make sure that you have begun to work successfully with annoyance before you attempt to apply the methods in this book to real anger. Steps three and four—compassion and softening around pain—may be useful in helping to deal with anger. But seek the help of a professional therapist if your anger affects your actions, until you can learn to control it on your own.

On Angst

If your tendency when hurt or frustrated is to attribute the blame to yourself ("I shouldn't have been there or said that" or "I don't know why, but it must be my fault" or, in inappropriate situations, "I'm sorry!"), then you are likely to be discouraged, depressive, and angst-ridden (*angst* is a German word for the emotion that includes, in varying mixtures, dread, depression, anxiety, and meaninglessness). Since angst, like anger, is a difficult and painful emotion to deal with, requiring hefty doses of compassion, we'll work more with it in steps three and four.

NEURAL NAVIGATION

What are some of the more likely elements that you might find in a neighborhood? Streets and stores, highways, and alleyways. Perhaps a mall, perhaps a business park. A tunnel to facilitate traffic flow, a pond or swamp that requires a detour, and lots of dead ends to block your way—if you don't know how to avoid them. Of course, once you have a sense of what you might find, and where, you can navigate your way around with speed and skill. We've just identified and discussed some of the more common denizens likely to be found in most neural neighborhoods, so it's time to start mapping out your own.

Labeling Thoughts Exercise

Here's a simple exercise that you can do for a few moments at a time or throughout an entire day. It will help you learn to treat thoughts as objects, by labeling them. Imagine that you are a bird-watcher. "Oh, there goes a yellow-bellied sapsucker." Then you would turn your attention back onto the sky. "Ah yes, there's a brown-headed cowbird." Simply try to label any thought or path as soon as you notice it. Once you've noticed and labeled a thought, just look around the horizon of your inner sky. Anything else to notice and label?

Some thoughts seem to grab your mental attention and hold onto it. We call these—surprise!—*grabby thoughts*, and we'll discuss them in a moment. For now, if you get grabbed by a thought, just label it. "Oh, a grabby thought. An anger-at-my-noisy-neighbor grabby thought." And try turning your attention onto your breath for a moment, to break the thought's hold on you by using breath focus to dissipate the fight-or-flight response that the grabby thought has triggered. Don't spend much time with this, although it's a useful exercise, and one that you can always return to. Instead, read on and investigate your top ten thoughts.

Thought Watching: Your Top Ten

Most of us have lots of thoughts, including quite a few that are less than welcome, but only a limited number repeat themselves with regularity. Like a radio station with a playlist, everyone has his or her own top ten problem thoughts. Unfortunately, though they may occur often, they are not always easy to spot or to anticipate.

Unpleasant physical situations and real-life scenarios, like waiting on the supermarket line or sitting in the dentist's chair, are generally easy to identify in advance. But troublesome thoughts and emotions are subtler and sneakier. They often seem to explode into consciousness, without hint or forewarning. Yet many of our most troublesome beliefs, biases, fears, desires, angsts, and angers are the result of long-standing neural paths, and with just a little bit of work, we can learn how to see them coming before they hit the fan.

Please take a moment and see if you can list some of the thoughts that most often run through your mind (don't worry about the order—this isn't really a popularity contest). Here's an example of the type of list we're talking about:

■   upset by politics

■   anger over _____: "They shouldn't treat me like that!"

■   generalized anger feelings, not specific

■   sex daydreams

■   planning thoughts about the new _____ project

■   self-talk: concern about money; then self-criticism self-talk ("I don't work hard enough."), then awfulizing ("I'll be living on the street.")

Now try doing your own list. Include, if appropriate, thought chains and self-talk comments, like the one in the example.

The Top Ten Draw-a-Breath Exercise

Now that you've consciously identified some of the more obvious inhabitants of your neural network, take a few more moments to literally draw your breath on paper. While drawing, if a thought (or self-talk or thought chain) should intrude, jot down a letter or two to symbolize it, then return to drawing your breath. This exercise may help you to identify mental objects that don't come quite so easily to your conscious mind. Here's an example.

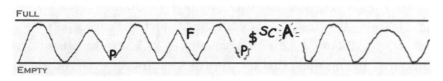

What does this chart represent? After a few breaths, a planning thought (P) almost disrupts the breath drawing, but not quite. After a few more breaths, a vague food thought (F) appears for a second, but doesn't interfere with the task.

Then a more intense planning thought (P) arises, leads to a worry about money ($), and—uh-oh—this person gets grabbed by the money worry. Her breath is forgotten (ragged line). When she eventually notices that she's stopped drawing her breath, there's a microsecond of perception—"I lost my breath focus" (not marked, it happens too fast). This is instantaneously followed by a few moments of self-criticism (SC)—"I've got the attention span of a fruit fly. I'm no good at anything"—leading to an angsty episode (A), in which the strong emotion provides an excellent additional distraction from the chosen task, and the person entirely forgets about the drawing of the breath.

Eventually, she realizes that any further investment in self-criticism is just keeping her from the breath drawing. She exhales (sighs?), and halfway through that out-breath, starts drawing again. Later, reviewing the chart, she can see a grabby neural path: planning thought to money worry, which triggers a fight-or-flight response, then a self-criticism leading to an angst emotion.

Why Do Some Thoughts Grab You?

What do you think of the typeface used in this book? Unless you're a book designer, you probably don't have strong thoughts about the subject. In other words, the thought of the typeface neither triggers the fight-or-flight response nor stimulates any particular self-talk leading to that response.

Grabby thoughts, on the other hand, or the grabby neural paths that they trigger, are paths that end in a stimulation of the fight-or-flight response and thus produce an emotion. In addition, grabby thoughts travel well-established, much practiced pathways. As we've discussed, a well-developed path has the quality of automaticity, meaning that it can rush from trigger event or trigger thought to emotion too swiftly to see. And if it happens too swiftly to see, it probably also happens too quickly to do anything about it—unless you're already prepared for it.

More "Grabbiness"—Tell Me No Stories

Grabby thoughts or paths are often the result of a mental or physical event that stimulates self-talk. The mind begins to tell you a story, and it's a scary story, a story that makes you angry, or a sad, angst-ridden story. When you are able to stay focused on the event itself, and don't allow yourself to get carried away by the story, your experience is quite different and usually much more manageable (less grabbed, that is).

The Usual Suspects

Once you've identified some of those top ten problem thoughts (or thought chains, or self-talk thoughts), you're ready to start navigating your neural network. Remember that the specific type of neural path doesn't matter. You can use breath focus to intervene with a fight-or-flight response whether it's caused by an event, a thought, self-talk, a thought chain, or any combination of the above. To do this, all you need are these two crucial elements:

- The ability to identify the thought or path before it hits the fan—that is, before it triggers the fight-or-flight response

- Enough mental muscle to refocus your attention onto the breath

Following is an excellent strategy for dealing with the less virulent members of your top ten problem thoughts. Although it won't work for really difficult thoughts or paths (unless you've practiced it long and hard), it can give near-instant relief from some of the repeated mental annoyances that, like mosquitos on a summer eve, or those ever-present dandelions in the tomato patch, plague you relentlessly even though they may do little permanent damage.

DEAD ENDS

Imagine that you're driving crosstown, and you see a dead-end sign. You don't agonize over whether you want to drive into the dead end—you know that you don't; it's already been decided that you're on your way elsewhere. And you don't start scrabbling around for the map—you know very well that the dead end won't get you where you want to go. You instantly know: don't go there.

Just Don't Go There

You also know that you may see another one (dead ends are like that, all over the place when you're in a hurry) or that you are likely to pass by the same sign again and again in your neighborhood travels. But you know just what to do as soon as you see it, whether it's the same sign or a new one: just don't go there! Likewise, there are thoughts—and paths they trigger—that are just crying out for a highly visible, if mental, dead-end sign.

Dead-End Thoughts and Paths

The analogy of the dead-end can help you deal with repetitive thoughts that are painful or otherwise unuseful. Dead-end thoughts, and the dead-end neural paths that they trigger, are thoughts and paths that you can:

1. Identify as probably being unwanted.

2. Investigate and evaluate further, if necessary.

3. Classify as being unuseful.

4. Then avoid them. If, for some reason, you feel like going down a dead-end, you can. But then it's your *choice*, not just a habitual reaction to an old, unuseful, but well-trod path.

Automatic Dead Ends

In a way, one could say that the dead-end treatment is using the too-swift-to-see or automaticity phenomenon in a positive way. That is, you make the new path—from perception of preidentified dead-end event or thought to breath focus—into such a no-brainer, so automatic, that it's possible to instantaneously change your focus as soon as you spot that dead-end event or thought.

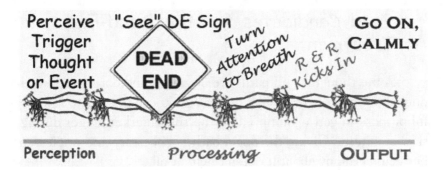

Perceive Trigger Thought or Event / "See" DE Sign / DEAD END / Turn Attention to Breath / R & R Kicks In / GO ON, CALMLY

Perception   *Processing*   OUTPUT

Isn't That Repression? Or Denial?

We are not Pollyanna types. Much of our work involves people in painful circumstances, and we don't want to sugarcoat the difficulties and stresses of human life. On the other hand, much of the mental distress you experience is caused by a limited number of repetitive thoughts, whose repetition is unuseful at best and self-hating at worst. These are the dead-end thoughts and the dead-end paths that they trigger.

This is *very* different from denial (pretending that the thought does not exist) or repression (trying to keep an important if unpleasant thought out of conscious awareness). The entire point of the dead-end thought exercise is that you have evaluated the thought, have decided that it is unuseful, and are choosing to avoid it, rather than attempting to ignore its existence.

This requires taking an honest look at the potential dead-end thought, what purpose (if any) it may serve, and why you want to remove it from your daily mental life. If you keep thinking about a disastrously ended love affair that is long past, it may be reasonable to treat it as a dead-end thought. But if you dead-end it as an excuse not to think about relationships at all—increasing your likelihood of repeating your mistakes—you may be abusing the strategy.

Good Candidates for the Dead-End Treatment

Some thoughts and paths are obvious candidates, such as the ones that you've already identified. You know that there's no useful purpose in getting annoyed on the supermarket line or during a slow commute. Giving the dog a bath is necessary and unpleasant, but being grumpy about it doesn't help at all.

Other potential dead-end thoughts or events require slightly more investigation, since we don't want to encourage the use of our dead-end strategy for avoidance or denial of issues that should be dealt with. For example, you may have thoughts about your physical appearance that cause a lot of self-criticism and even depression. Are these dead-end thoughts?

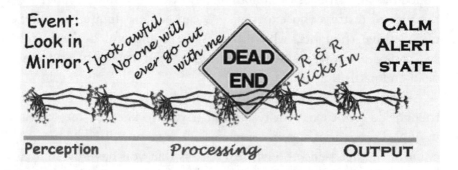

In general, a good set of questions, or criteria, for dead-end designation is the following:

1.   Is this an issue you can do anything about? If you have painful thoughts about something that happened in the past or about being too tall or too short, the answer is clearly no. Thoughts about being overweight? Thoughts about something that happened in the past but which you may repeat if you're not careful? Then the answer is yes, but...

2. Are you currently willing or planning or desperately needing to do anything about the issue? If you are overweight but *not* planning to diet, then this neural path may well be a good candidate for the dead-end treatment. Remember that you can always take a thought out of the dead-end category—if you decide to consider dieting, then a thought about your weight is no longer a dead-end thought but a potentially useful motivator. Of course, if you use the thought in a mean or self-hating way, it then goes back to being a dead-ender! If the boss's son annoys you, but you like your job, dead-end the thoughts of annoyance until you're ready to job hunt, then utilize them to lend wings to your search.

3. You can also temporarily assign a dead-end designation. For example, while working on deadline, worrying about your love life should probably be a dead-ender. In couples counseling, it surely shouldn't.

But the bottom line is this: Most of us already know what our dead-end thoughts are. Many of them have plagued us since childhood or adolescence. Please choose one of your most obvious candidates—preferably not your most painful one. Use a physical imperfection of yours or a colleague who annoys you by eating with his mouth open, rather than how you feel abandoned by your parents, since the dead-end strategy tends to work best with less serious candidates. Then start working on the following exercise for an instant improvement in your day-to-day mental state!

The Dead-End Exercise

Using the dead-end strategy is not very different from the real-life exercise you've already done. Just apply these steps:

1. Identify a dead-end candidate (which you already should have done).

2. Commit to using one or more breath-focus exercises to short-circuit the path that it usually triggers (hopefully, you already have enough mental muscle to do this).

3. Consciously bring the dead-end thought into your mind. Visualize a dead-end sign popping up, and refocus as soon as you see that dead-end sign, using the actual breath exercise that you've committed to (this creates a new neural path).

4. Do the visualization often enough so that the new neural path is strengthened.

5. Remember to use this same process whether you are bringing the dead-end thought into your mind on purpose, or whether it pops in on its own.

With repeated practice, it will become easier to use the dead-end strategy for any particular thought that you've chosen as a dead-end candidate. And each time you do this for a thought, it becomes easier to use the dead-end strategy on any different thought or path.

DEAD-END PREP: TOUGHER CUSTOMERS

We've requested that you start your practice of the dead-end strategy with an easy candidate. Eventually, you'll want to be able to use it with tougher customers, but don't be in a hurry to do so just yet. Instead, try these exercises that will help you to investigate the nature of desire, of fear, and of interpersonal relations. Practicing them will make it easier, eventually, to cope successfully with more painful or difficult thoughts, people, and situations of all types.

Desire Prep Exercise

Here's a slightly different, but very simple, kind of breathing exercise for you. Take a breath—not too deep—and hold it. Notice how after just a few seconds you start to want to breathe again. The longer you hold your breath, the more you want, and need, to exhale and take a new one. That's the simplest desire, hardwired into your brain since the first adventurous fish finned its way onto the beach.

As we've mentioned, many desires are hardwired into us, for what were originally very good reasons. Without food or water we'd die, without sexual attraction we'd die out, as a race, at least. This was all very well among our distant ancestors—until thought entered the picture, in the minds of *Homo sapiens*. Whereas previously, hunger or sexual-desire neural paths were triggered only by either hardwired responses based on actual need or on the actual perception of a food or sex object in the real world, these desires could now, in human brains, be triggered by nothing more than a fantasy, a ghost, a thought.

The next time you become aware of any mild desire— "Hmmm, I could use a sandwich" or "I think I'd like to read the paper for a while"—play with it. Instead of immediately seeking to satisfy the desire, whether need or greed, turn your attention to one of the breathing exercises. Just notice whether doing this affects your reaction to the desire. As you breathe, try also to focus in on the physical sensation of the desire rather than on any thoughts about it. Notice if the desire stimulates self-talk ("But I've been working for hours. I deserve a break"). If so, the breath focus should take your attention away from the story that your mind is telling you about the desire.

In this exercise, you're not necessarily trying to avoid the satisfaction of the desire. You're just investigating the nature of desire itself, as an object in the mind, rather than as some internal marching command that you must instantly obey.

Fear Prep Exercise

You can do a similar exercise with fear, although rather than spontaneously waiting for a fear to pop into your head, it's safer (more controllable) to choose one consciously—a nice, mild, manageable one. This is basically a version of the PONR Scan Exercise in step one, where you practiced short-circuiting your fight-or-flight response. In fact, most of these exercises have a number of similarities, since they are all based on the fact that focusing attention onto the breath defuses the fight-or-flight response.

In this case, it's the flight—the fear—response that needs to be short-circuited. So please

1. Consciously bring a mild fear into your awareness—a top ten fear would be great to work with if you have one that seems appropriate (not too intense).

2. Simultaneously, try to focus on the breathing exercise of your choice.

3. Observe any physical sensations that may arise.

4. If you feel the physical sensations approaching the point of no return—the PONR—and you start feeling anxious, turn your full attention back onto your breath until they subside.

Doing this may reduce the impact of the fear thought. But if this exercise seems difficult to do, try the following interpersonal exercises. Then, come back to your fear thought and apply what you've learned about split attention.

Interpersonal Exercise #1

This one will help to prepare you for some of the interpersonal work we'll be introducing in steps three and five. You'll need a TV or a radio.

1. Turn the channel or tuner to find a commentator that you neither like nor dislike, preferably a face or voice that you can't even identify, speaking on a subject that you don't care much about.

2. Do any of the breathing exercises as you listen, and practice dividing your attention between your breath and the words of the speaker.

3. You'll find that you can catch much of the content of the material, the gist of the argument or story, while still staying pretty well focused on your breath.

4. If you get "grabbed" by the speaker, turn more attention onto the breath as soon as you notice this.

5. If you stop hearing what the speaker is saying, put more attention on the speaker and less on your breath.

    Your goal is to identify and maintain the sense of what Freud called "evenly suspended attention."

Interpersonal Exercise #2

In this exercise you practice the same technique but with a live person, not a radio or TV. You may want to start out in a situation where a group of people is listening to someone speaking. Attempt to look as though all of your attention is going to the speaker, keeping your eyes on him or her (you'll find that looking at the bridge of his or her nose gives the impression, from all but the closest distances, of maintaining eye contact but is easier than actually doing so). Of course, you are actually splitting your attention between the speaker and your chosen breath-focus exercise. If you've got a pen and a clipboard, the draw-a-breath exercises work very nicely here, as long as no one else can see what you're writing!

Interpersonal Exercise #3

When you feel comfortable doing the second exercise—without getting caught—try doing the same thing in a one-on-one situation, splitting your attention between breath focus and the conversation. Naturally, you'll want to choose a conversation in which the content of the discussion is unimportant, and one in which you are not expected to respond with more than the occasional nod or "uh-huh."

Do this with a person who tends to talk more than he or she listens, and who is almost certain not to notice that you are not participating verbally. This is a great way to get a reputation as a good listener from people who like to talk. It's also a great way to avoid becoming bored or annoyed when you are listening to content that doesn't interest you—listening to a neighbor who loves to gossip about people you don't know or to a less-than-sensitive friend who has never noticed your total lack of interest in his favorite team sport.

As you listen with split attention, notice any self-talk, or thoughts, or story that arises. "How can he be so insensitive? Doesn't he know I hate football?" Just return your attention to the breath. With practice, this set of exercises can provide you with a wonderful tool for dealing with difficult or unpleasant interpersonal situations.

THE DEAD END TO END ALL DEAD ENDS

We've given you a lot of potentially difficult exercises in this chapter. Please don't let a slip—a lapse in your commitment, a few weeks of laziness, a failure to stick with an exercise, or the program itself—blossom into self-sabotage. Do you have a tendency to become discouraged or angst-ridden and give up on things when you feel frustrated or not fully successful ("I can't do this. I'm no good. I might as well—sigh—quit")? Or a tendency to turn frustration into anger ("This is stupid. I quit!")? If so, just allow yourself to recognize those angst and anger paths for the dead ends that they are. Take a deep breath, label that path with a big, diamond-shaped yellow sign, and don't go there!

Summing Up

Thoughts are objects, mental objects. Drawing their neural path diagrams helps to remind you of this. You can learn to manipulate mental objects, just as you do physical ones.

Some physical objects are light, convenient, and easy to manipulate. Others are heavy and hard to move. Like any habitual action, thought habits—strong and well-trodden neural paths—take energy and practice and commitment if you want to change them.

But it's doable, once you understand the strategies for it. And it's important. If you don't learn to control the neural paths that you've created in your past, you will continue to bring the past into your present, which will affect your future.

To a large extent, the quality of your life is dictated by where you put your mental attention. It's like living in any neighborhood. If you were to spend most of your time in low-class bars, at the dump, in the red-light district, or in dead-end mud and mire, the quality of your life would differ from how it would be if you spent most of your time at the community college, at the church, or in the homes of friends and family. With knowledge of your neural neighborhood and the mental muscle to navigate it, the choice of where to spend your limited and valuable time becomes yours.

CHAPTER 3

Step Three

Compassion:
Healing
the Hurt Spots

Here's what we've covered so far:

- In the introduction, you learned about neural paths, mental muscle, and the fight-or-flight and relax-and-release responses.

- In step one, you studied breath techniques for building mental muscle; then you applied some of them to a real-life situation.

- In step two, you learned to combine mental muscle with your knowledge of neural paths to start coping with low-intensity variations of the issues that affect all of us: fear, anger, desire.

All of the techniques you've used up to now can be described as *coping skills*. A problem arises, and you use a breathing technique to cope with it—by turning your attention away from the problem thought or path, then defusing the fight-or-flight response by refocusing your attention onto the breath. In effect, you've been learning to shift your brain into neutral gear. Shifting your car into neutral disengages the power of the engine from the wheels. Using these skills helps you to "disengage" the power of the fight-or-flight response from your thoughts.

Once a car is in neutral gear, you can then put it into any other gear—forward or reverse, fast or slow. Likewise, when you've defused the fight-or-flight response, you can then turn your attention in whatever direction you choose. This allows you to make wise choices on where to place your mental attention (and as the Buddhist teacher and writer Thich Nhat Hanh puts it, "If you want to have a nice garden, don't water the weeds!").

BEYOND COPING

In steps three and four, we will present more advanced techniques for working with those severe problems and pains that cannot simply be coped with, dead-ended and turned away from, or breathed through. For example, it may be healthy to turn attention away from an annoying habit of an aging parent but unhealthy to deny the reality of advancing senility, painful though that reality may be. Although it's not always easy, by learning to develop the compassion response and learning to soften around pain, you'll eventually be able to work more skillfully with some of the most basic and powerful afflictions inherent in the human condition.

A SOMEWHAT ARBITRARY CHOICE

The decision to place compassion work in step three and softening-around-pain work in step four was somewhat arbitrary. It may be you'll find that softening around pain (step four) will help you prepare for compassion work. Both steps are essential and equally important, so please keep reading and follow our suggestions if step three is difficult for you.

WARNING: MAINTAIN MENTAL MUSCULATURE!

As you begin to work with the more advanced techniques, please remember that no technique will work if you do not maintain your mental muscle. Unfortunately, mental muscle is not a thing that you achieve or obtain once, then own forever, like a law degree or a rowing machine. It's much more akin to staying in physical shape, just as even an experienced baseball player, after decades of life as a couch potato, will not be able to bat, catch, or run very well—even though he or she may still *understand* how to do those things. In a very real way, mental muscle is the basic element on which the entire neural path therapy method is built. This is such an important topic that we'd like to expand upon it for a moment.

THE NEURAL PATH THERAPY PYRAMID

We (or at least the birds among us) may like to visualize the neural path therapy method as a pyramid.

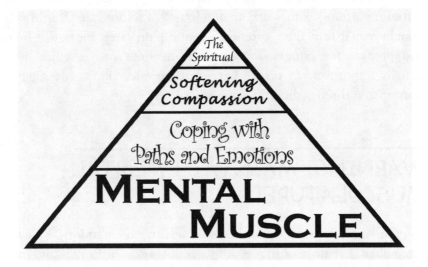

The base of the pyramid—representing the underpinnings of the method—is composed of mental muscle: lots of it. If this were a food pyramid, the base would be whole grains and fruits and vegetables—stuff that's really good for you, and thus important to ingest in massive quantities.

The next level of the pyramid involves applying that mental muscle toward coping with various thoughts, paths, self-talk processes, and emotional responses. A smaller (and more psychologically subtle) level is that of compassion and softening around pain —learning to face the world with compassion and without hardening yourself unnecessarily. And the topmost, smallest section—one which only a few of us may actually integrate into our lives—involves going beyond the steps, to the pinnacle from which we look at the philosophical and spiritual implications of the neural path therapy method.

Mental Muscle: The Bottom Line

No matter how exalted the step, it is mental muscle upon which the entire edifice rests. That's because mental muscle is what you must use to refocus mental attention, whether you are refocusing it onto the breath (steps one and two), onto compassion (step three), onto softening around pain (step four), or onto the highest objects of spiritual awareness (beyond the steps). So please continue to practice both the mental muscle breathing exercises in step one, as well as their real-life applications as described in step two.

Putting It All Together: The Top Lines

It may seem paradoxical, but for some of us (the more analytical types), learning about the top of the pyramid—that is, how the lower levels of the neural path therapy method connect to the philosophical and spiritual levels—may help provide understanding and motivation. So please don't think that you have to master each exercise in the earlier steps before reading about the later ones.

ANGER, ANGST, DESIRE, AND ... COMPASSION?

On page 66, we discussed our belief that there are a few very general pathways or strategies for going through life. Some people prefer to attribute pain or problems to a hostile world, to blame others for their suffering—they subscribe to a belligerent and vengeful worldview. Others blame themselves for any problem, withdrawing and curling up with an apology—they subscribe to a depressive, guilty worldview. A few people go through life in acquisition mode—mainly concerned with satisfying appetites, whether it is food, sex, money, or status that is craved. Most people embody some combination of these strategies for embracing the world: a main course of anger with a side of appetite, or a favored tendency toward angst with a bit of desire and occasional anger. No matter which worldview or worldview combination you embody, it is reflected in the choice of events and thoughts that trigger your neural paths, reflected in the way you self-talk, reflected in which of the hardwired paths (fight, flight, need) that are activated. Thus your worldview tends to direct your neural paths to end in anger, in angst, in desire.

But there is another way, the way of the kind and generous neighbor, the way of a Mother Teresa or a Dalai Lama, the way of those who act as their brother's or sister's keeper. How is it that some people face the vicissitudes of life with compassion rather than with anger, acquisitiveness, or angst?

The Compassion Response

The first two life strategies can be tied, of course, to the anger (fight) and angst (flight) responses, and the third to the hardwired needs for food, sex, and security. Perhaps the fourth—the path of compassion—is based on yet another ancient hardwired response: the instinctual protective love of a mother or father for the offspring, which goes back to the days of the later dinosaurs and earlier birds. It may also be related to the attachment of individuals to the group that exists among animals that naturally live in groups, such as dogs or chimpanzees. Whatever its origin, we believe that the compassion response is hardwired within people, and you can learn to access it at will, no matter how blocked it may be at first. Doing so can change your life.

A Note on Anger and Compassion

Is your tendency to follow the path of anger more often than the path of angst? Then step three may be especially difficult for you, since anger is the opposite of compassion. If this is true for you, please read step three anyway, and try the exercises. Should they be frustrating, go on to step four and work with softening around pain. Then return to step three, and you will likely find it to be more accessible. Please understand the later steps of this program are more subtle, more difficult, and will take longer to master than the earlier ones. Don't be hard on yourself, just because they seem hard.

What Is Compassion?

Compassion might be called a type of love, but it is easiest to define by what it is not. It involves love—self-love—for yourself, without self-pity or narcissism, without the need to be perfect. It involves love for others, without eroticism, pity, the hope that they will make you look good, or any other expectation of return.

The Difference Between Compassion and Pity

It's possible to differentiate compassion from pity by this criteria: in pity, there is an element of fear for yourself. You see the accident victim, and your feelings of empathy are tinged with fear for yourself ("Gee, that could have happened to me—I'm glad it didn't and sure hope that it doesn't"). In compassion, there is a wry acceptance of the human condition that we all share—that we are all basically helpless in the face of fate—and no need or attempt to distance the negative events by making them something that happens to someone else.

Self-Love Without Narcissism

Narcissus was the youth of Greek mythology who fell in love with his own reflection. The personality trait or (in extreme form) personality disorder called *narcissism* involves being excessively interested in your reflection, that is, in how you appear to others. The narcissist also has a strong need for admiration or adulation and lacks empathy—the ability to recognize that others have feelings or needs just as he or she does. Instead, other people are objects to the narcissist—fashion accessories (a lovely young wife, a perfect child) used to aggrandize the narcissist in his or her own eyes or in the eyes of others. Narcissists often tend to appear to have a very exalted view of themselves, which might be interpreted as a tremendous amount of self-love. But does having compassion for the self make you narcissistic?

Often, buried deeply under a narcissistic exterior, beneath loads of narcissistic self-talk in neural paths ("Not enough people looked at me today. Better spend the evening at the gym"), the narcissist feels inadequate or inferior. True compassion toward the self—self-love—involves loving yourself regardless of external appearance or financial or social worth—and is the opposite of, and the antidote to, narcissism.

Self-Love Without Self-Pity

Loving yourself is subtly different from feeling sorry for yourself, which we generally refer to as self-pity. Self-pity ("Oh, poor me") is often a well-established neural path, triggered by events or thoughts of pain or frustration that lead to self-pitying self-talk, which then triggers a flight response and ends with an emotion of angst. It often results in immobilization, as your energy goes into feeling sorry for yourself rather than into action to deal with the pain or frustration. This is just another variation of the "I can't do this; I'm no good; I guess I'll just quit" path that we've already discussed a number of times. The self-compassion exercises later in this chapter will help you deal with this issue if it arises for you. On the positive side, those who feel angst often find it easier to hone their sense of compassion than do those for whom anger is the predominant path.

THE FEEL OF COMPASSION

In earlier steps, you explored the physical and mental sensations of the fight-or-flight response as you approach the point of no return and their attendant emotions of anger and fear. You also, in the desire prep exercise at the end of step two, observed and played with the sensation of mild desire. Now it's time to investigate the more subtle experience of compassion.

Defining compassion in words may be difficult, but identifying the sensation of compassion is less so. It's a bit like (if you'll pardon the comparison) what Supreme Court Justice Potter Stewart said of pornography: that he could not define it, but "I know it when I see it." You know compassion when you feel it. As a hardwired response, it's somewhat similar to the R & R response, except that it does not follow the fight-or-flight response. A feeling of compassion is often described as a warm, melting, softening sensation, perhaps accompanied by an "ooooh..." or "awwww..." vocalization and is triggered in most of us by the sight or thought of a small, appealing, helpless creature. A head and eyes that are large relative to the creature's size—as in a baby—will help to elicit the compassion response.

This sense of selfless love for the compassion object—often a human infant of the viewer's family or clan—was clearly an adaptive mechanism to help bring the infant safely through the dangers and needs of childhood. The following exercise will help you to identify this important emotion, which you need to apply, not just to babies and large-eyed velvet paintings, but to yourself.

The Compassion Response Exercise

This exercise is designed to help you identify the general compassion response, rather than a compassion response directed toward yourself or any particular other.

1. Spend a moment with your favorite breathing exercise.

2. When you feel relaxed, bring an image that you think may elicit a sense of compassion into your mind. For many people, a beloved childhood pet (especially a kitten or puppy) is a good compassion object. It may seem silly, but some people find that the image of the sickly, helpless extraterrestrial ET in the movie of the same name is a good compassion object (the design of the alien was clearly chosen to elicit the viewer's compassion, with its large head and oversize eyes and weak, spindly appendages).

3. Look inside to perceive physical sensations of the compassion response, such as warmth in the center of your body, a melting feeling, a silent "awwww" vocalization. If your mental image brings up many thoughts or paths other than compassion, you may need to try another image. Or you can simply notice, "Ahhh, that's just my mind telling stories again..." and return your attention to the compassion object.

4. If the first thought that you attempted to use to trigger the compassion response did not seem to work, just try another one. Perhaps a character from fiction (Tiny Tim, of Charles Dickens's *Christmas Carol*, is a classic compassion object) or a scene from a movie might do it. The image of the *Pieta* (a grieving Mary holding the body of her dead son) is often a good compassion object

for people of the Christian faith or for anyone who can feel the power of a great work of art. It may be that for some of us, especially the birds, a visual image—a photo or picture—will make it easier to stimulate the compassion response. Sadly, it's not too hard to find a tragic image of a young child, in these warlike days, which just proves how crucial it is to develop compassion.

If the above exercise seemed difficult, please continue on to these others. If they too seem hard, you may want to work with the softening-around-pain exercises in step four before returning to this compassion work.

Breathing from the Heart

This sensation-based general compassion exercise may work best for the barnacles amongst us.

1. As before, spend a moment or two with your favorite breathing exercise.

2. Once you feel relaxed, pretend (all anatomical knowledge aside) that your breath—rather than passing in and out from your lungs—is moving into and out of your heart. Try to *feel* this happening, not see it.

Compassion Exercise: The Sigh Breath

The bats in our midst may find this general compassion exercise easiest to focus on.

1. Do a moment or two of your favorite breathing exercise.

2. Then change each breath into a sigh. In a sigh, the inhale is usually deep and through either the nose or the mouth. The exhale is through the mouth, nose closed, with a slight (even imperceptible) "haaaaa" or "aaaaaah" vocalization.

3. Make a conscious attempt to relax your body on each out-breath, as you sigh.

Self-Compassion Exercise #1

Once you are able to identify the compassion response to some extent, try applying some compassion to yourself with this exercise.

1. Picture yourself as a small child at the youngest age that you can remember. Visualize your child-self as clearly as possible.

2. Then try to create a compassion response while picturing that small child-self. Wrap your arms around yourself, or at least place one hand over the other in a loving, compassionate way. In your mind's eye, see yourself as an adult hugging your child-self.

3. If feelings or thoughts other than love and compassion enter (especially judgmental thoughts, such as "I don't deserve this" or "A kid's gotta be tough"), gently return your mind to thoughts of love and compassion for your child-self.

Self-Compassion Exercise #2

This exercise is a continuation of the first, but unless the first self-compassion exercise seemed really easy, repeat #1 a few times before moving on to this one.

1. Picture yourself as an older child and do what you did in the previous exercise. Don't forget to hug yourself, at least in your mind.

2. Then picture yourself at puberty (an age where we all especially need compassion and hugs) and do the exercise. Then picture yourself again in steps of five or ten years until you are picturing yourself at your present age.

3. Now do the same thing you've been doing for your younger selves—bathe yourself in love and compassion while hugging yourself. Only this time, do it right now, with your own arms wrapped lovingly around yourself.

COMPASSION AND SELF-ACCEPTANCE

For many of us, compassionate feelings for ourselves at any age do not come easily, and we may even criticize ourselves for not being able to do the previous compassion exercises perfectly enough. That's why developing a sense of compassion must lie at the heart of any self-help regimen, including this one. Without it, the neural path therapy method is all too likely to become just another activity that you do "wrong," or "don't do enough," or "should be attaining quicker results" from. Yet two seeming paradoxes can make it difficult to avoid being self-critical when working on a self-help program.

Swamps Versus Alligators

You've probably heard the old complaint, "It's hard to drain the swamp when you're up to your rear in alligators." Another aphorism also applies: "You can't learn to swim while the boat is sinking." They are both true, of course. One of the great paradoxes of therapy—whether done with a professional or on your own—is that you need to build skills to work with the difficult issues that brought you there in the first place, yet it's hard to stay focused on building those skills while problem issues are sapping your self-esteem and mental energy.

This is why we've emphasized the mental muscle exercises in step one—the basic building blocks of the neural path therapy method—so heavily. By practicing the exercises before you attempt to use them in real life, and then by using the exercises in real-life but low-stakes situations, you slowly begin to drain the swamp of an unruly mind, while ignoring the alligators. Those overgrown lizards (your more difficult or painful problems) will still be there when you feel ready to face them, this time with the tools of mental muscle, compassion, and softening around pain.

Change Versus Acceptance

Another paradox is that for therapy to succeed, you—the client—need to have enough compassion to accept yourself as you are, no matter how much you want—or need—to change. As with so many things, it's a balancing act. Perhaps a good analogy is that you love a kitten or puppy in spite of its babyish behavior—peeing on the rug, chewing your slippers, digging in the orchid pot. You know that it is a baby animal. You know that with proper training, it will grow and change. You want those changes to occur, yet you love the little creature (exasperated though you may be sometimes during the training process).

Similarly, you must have compassion for where you are and who you are now, understanding that you find yourself in this place because of many elements in your past. Many of these—ranging from the evolutionary biology that provides your hardwired neural paths to the parenting you received to the culture that you live in—have been far beyond your individual control. So the only rational reaction to your current plight is to accept yourself with compassion while striving diligently to change for the better.

Self-Soothing Exercise

If you just can't seem to locate any shred of compassion in your makeup, try this simple exercise.

1. Prepare to do something small but kind for yourself: take a warm bath, eat a favorite food (but not something so indulgent that you'll criticize yourself for eating it), spend an extra half hour with an old friend of a book.

2. Begin with a few minutes of breathing exercise. Then give yourself the little gift as you would give it to a treasured friend. Midway during the bath, or the dessert, or the reading, turn your attention onto your breath again.

3. If this exercise makes you feel sad, it may be that you are realizing the lack of compassion you hold for yourself. If that's the case, please turn back to self-compassion exercise #1 (page 94). You are still the child who needs and *deserves* love and compassion—as much as any appealing puppy or cuddly kitten—and you have the ability to give it to yourself, right now.

In many ways, self-compassion is not so different from acting as a friend to yourself. Practice that act with sincerity and without self-criticism, and you may find that the compassion response develops by itself.

COMPASSION AND INTERPERSONAL RELATIONS

If you've had any success in identifying the compassion response and applying it to yourself, it's time to try applying it to others. In fact, even if you haven't been able to muster up much self-love, try the following exercises, since you may find it easier to be compassionate with others than with yourself. In fact, it may be easiest to be compassionate toward those you don't know very well, as illustrated by the following exercise.

About the I-Thou and the I-It

Jewish theologian Martin Buber coined the term "I-Thou," to indicate a relationship in which one person (the "I") relates to another person (the "Thou") with the understanding that the other has as many feelings and needs, fears and desires, as the first person does, and as much right to pursue them. Buber contrasts this with the "I-It" relationship, in which you act as though the other person is mostly an object, whose principal purpose in life is to help you gain satisfaction.

A person who behaves this way with everyone—friends, relatives, lovers—is called, as you remember, a narcissist. But most of us, if honest, must ask ourselves how often (especially when we're in a hurry) does a store clerk or a gas station attendant seem to be a real, complete person with his or her own history and feelings? When someone cuts ahead of you on line, do you usually perceive him or her as a person who has problems, fears, and needs, just as you do, or is he or she just some "impolite jerk" getting between you and the candy counter? Can you really see that the beautiful woman or hunky man walking across the street has a full and complete life of her or his own, and does not just exist as an object for your visual (or perhaps fantasized sexual) gratification?

The I-Thou Compassion Exercise

1. Begin by choosing someone whom you neither like nor dislike: a supermarket cashier, neighbor, or business acquaintance to whom you usually *don't* relate.

2. Try to perceive this person as a "thou" instead of an "it."

3. When you are able to see a "neutral person" as a thou, try doing the same exercise with someone whom you have a very mild dislike for, or bias against.

After practicing on a variety of neutral experimental subjects, you can begin to practice the I-Thou exercise on someone whom you might normally tend to dislike because of old biases or beliefs. Over time, you'll eventually be able to do this with a surly waiter, a somewhat aggressive panhandler, or perhaps even a relatively moderate politician not from the party of your choice.

The Shared-Breath Compassion Exercise

This enormously powerful exercise is often used by those who work with sick or dying patients, but you can do it with anyone whom you happen to be with, even a pet. You simply choose a person and match your breath rate to his or hers, in for in, out for out. It's easiest to do, at first, if you do not need to talk or interact with the person whom you are trying to breathe with. There's no reason to let the other person know what you're doing.

1. Begin by splitting your attention between your "breather" and your own breath, without trying to match breathing rates consciously.

2. When you feel relaxed, start to observe the ins and outs of your breather's breath, and start matching the rate.

Once you have practiced doing this exercise in a situation in which no response is required of you, try it during a casual, low-stakes conversation with a friend. Try to balance your attention between the matching of your breath rates and any conversation, eye contact, or perception of body language that may occur or be expected of you. If you lose track of your friend's breath, simply start over, with neither self-criticism nor hesitation.

The Mutual Shared-Breath Exercise

This is a great exercise to share with a loved one or an old friend. Allow one person to be the "designated breather" and the other to be the "designated breath follower." If you can do this while maintaining eye contact, it can be a very powerful bonding experience. An even more advanced technique would be for both of you try to match the other's breath rate. Try not to force the other person to breath at your tempo, but rather mutually, slowly, try to find a good speed that suits you both.

Summing Up

Identifying and enhancing the compassion response is crucial to the therapy process, yet it is very difficult for many of us. Some of the reasons for this may become clearer when you consider the material in step five. But for now, if you find it difficult to work with compassion, please do two things. Notice, with a wry smile, the irony of being uncompassionate with yourself for not being able to work with compassion. And be at least compassionate enough with yourself to continue on to step four. The act of learning to soften around pain may make step three easier to return to and work with.

CHAPTER 4

Step Four

Softening Around Pain: When Life Is Hard

Here's what you've accomplished:

- In step one, you learned to build mental muscle so that you could refocus your mental attention onto your breath (which of course stimulates the R & R response and thus short-circuits the fight-or-flight response).

- In step two, you learned to identify a variety of neural paths on which to apply the above set of techniques. This, we hope, allowed you to begin coping better with some of your less useful (or dead-end) paths.

- In step three, you began to investigate the hardwired but often elusive pathway that we call the compassion response.

In this step, you'll start working on a new way to relate to one of the planet's oldest and most intractable problems: pain.

JUST A STUBBED TOE?

Say you walk into a dark room and stub your toe on a chair that's been left in the middle of the floor. For many people, the first reaction is anger, with its desire to blame or lash out. Others crumple in upon themselves, crying (or feeling like it). As in so many things, a basic tendency toward anger or angst helps to direct your reaction to an event. But either way, pain often engenders a tightening or hardening of the body, a gritting of the teeth.

TYPES OF PAIN

There are many types of pain. What they all have in common is that softening around them works, if you can do it. Since the basic softening-around-pain technique is similar, regardless of the type of pain, in step four we will alternate descriptive or informational content with the actual exercises, rather than (as in most of the other steps) tending to start with description, before moving on to exercises.

You can work with pain on the level of the body (physical pain) or on the level of the mind (which involves both thoughts that cause mental pain and thoughts about physical pain). Let's begin with an investigation of physical pain, since it's something that everyone has already experienced.

About Physical Pain

Physical pain can be as unexpected and acute as a stubbed toe or as chronic and predictable as a bad back. No matter what causes it, when you really investigate pain you find that the stories that your mind tells you about pain—your self-talk on the subject—are likely to make it worse. The following exercises may help you to work more skillfully with pain, but make sure that you only use them in safe ways. If you may possibly need medical care for a pain—by all means, get it! You should only use these exercises with pain that clearly requires no immediate medical attention. We'll begin with intentional (elective) pain—not because we are sadists but because it provides an easier way to investigate pain than waiting for the accidental variety to happen.

Acceptance Versus Refocusing

In a number of the exercises in steps one and two, we simply asked you to refocus your attention onto your breath. This works quite well on less difficult or painful issues. But in more serious scenarios, you may not be able to eliminate pain in body or mind by simple refocusing. In these situations, the acceptance skills—compassion and softening around pain—will be more useful. The desensitization split-attention exercises toward the end of this chapter may also help.

You may ask, "When do I just refocus, and when do I accept pain?" As with the question "What is a good dead-end thought?" there is a difficult and subtle distinction, akin to the well-known Serenity Prayer (used by AA members, and often attributed in this wording to theologian Reinhold Niebuhr, although its origin is disputed and may date back two millennia):

"God, give us grace to accept with serenity the things that cannot be changed, courage to change the things which should be changed, and the wisdom to distinguish the one from the other."

Compassion, Not Competition

Since it's almost impossible not to tighten around severe pain without lots of practice, these exercises work with moderate and self-controlled doses of discomfort. And remember, they are not to be performed competitively, with much gritting of teeth, but with gentleness and compassion. If you find yourself trying to "tough these out," perhaps you'd better return to step three and work on compassion for a while.

Response-to-Pain Exercise

There are safe—if not necessarily pleasant—ways to easily play with the sensation of pain. Please don't do this one if you suffer from diabetes or any other illness that would impair circulation or involve sensitivity of the feet.

1. While barefooted, gently kick a hard object—your desk or the table leg—not hard enough to do any damage or to cause more than a second's mild pain.

2. Now act out, in both mind and body, an exaggerated reaction that takes one of two forms—either anger (grit your teeth, clench your fists, and mutter or yell, "Who left that *&% desk there?") or angst (grit your teeth, hunch your shoulders, moan "Owww!" and perhaps fake a tear or two).

Investigate Your Reaction

Think about which response came more naturally to you. This is very likely the way you react to most pain. Since we've all experienced pains of various sorts since infancy, our reactions to it have become automatic—too swift to see, and pretty much occurring below the level of conscious thought.

In our culture, male children are often taught to tough it out in situations of physical pain, so (as always when talking of gender differences, this is a nothing but a generalization) older male children and men often have more difficulty with softening around pain than women do. But there is also a gender-free hardwired component that contributes to the automaticity of our "hardening" reaction to pain, honed over hundreds of millions of years by the physical trials and tribulations of our forebears.

Like a Fistful of Thorns

In the distant past, when pain was likely to be caused by the bite of a hostile or hungry beast, an automatic reaction of tightening the body in preparation for fight or flight may have been a useful response. In today's world, with a plethora of more subtle and more chronic discomforts, this is often less true. Imagine holding a handful of rose stems, each laden with sharp thorns, in your hand. Grasp the stems tightly and the thorns pierce your flesh. But if you allow them to lie loose on your palm, they barely prick the skin at all.

Obviously, some pains require an immediate response—if you lean against a hot stove, the sooner you can move, the better. But for many sources of modern pain, our reaction to the pain only worsens it, as we clench our fist more tightly around the thorny branches. That's what softening to pain is all about.

Softening Around Pain Exercise

1. Now repeat the last exercise—a carefully modulated barefoot kick to an unyielding object.

2. This time, as soon as you perceive the pain in your toe, use mental muscle to refocus your attention onto your breath in your favorite breathing exercise.

3. At the same time, consciously relax your shoulders, your jaw, the muscles of your stomach, and your hands (the places most likely to tense up in this situation).

4. Since your toe should be hurting (just a little), your attention will be split between the physical sensation of pain and your breath.

    Did this exercise affect your experience of the pain in any way?

Symbolic Tension: The Hard Spot

Many people find that they carry a great deal of their pain tension in a single specific spot (usually shoulders, stomach, jaw, or hands, with shoulders being the most common). If this seems to be true for you, practice relaxing that one area of your body, so that you can do it instantly, and on command. You may find that simply relaxing that one area will help to symbolize softening around pain as you do the following exercises.

Acceptance Versus Emergency

People often treat the sensation of pain as an emergency—as though something must be done about it, right away. And as we've pointed out, some pain requires immediate action. But in other cases, it can be instructive to make a conscious decision not to react to pain. Rather, accept it and simply experience it for a moment. The following exercise, strange though it may seem, will help you to explore this.

The Hot Sauce Exercise

Although overuse of hot sauce or chile peppers can be momentarily unpleasant, it is not physically harmful, and it's an experience of limited duration. So it's a good way to practice softening around pain. If you are not a fan of spicy food, choose your condiment carefully, as even a single drop of some of the extreme hot products (whose names, like "Suicide Sauce" or "Insanely Hot Salsa," give clear warning) can be excruciating to nonaficionados.

1. Prepare an appropriate amount of hot sauce in a teaspoon— perhaps half again as much as you'd normally consider eating by itself. If you like hot stuff, this will be easy to judge. If not, try a single drop of a mild hot sauce (your local supermarket sells clearly labeled bottles of this for less than a dollar).

2. Spend a moment with your favorite breathing exercise, then take the hot sauce into your mouth (don't just swallow it).

3. Notice the sensation of pain. Then try to return your attention to the breath.

4. If you've administered a proper dosage of hotness, you will want to act. To rush for a glass of ice water. To be angry at this book or at yourself ("What a dumb exercise!"). To cry? Your body or jaw may tense up. Instead, just notice your thoughts, and try to return your attention to the breath.

5. Continue to divide your attention between the breath, the desire to act to reduce the hotness, and the sensation of hotness itself, until the sensations subside.

6. If you end up running for the ice water, this exercise can still be a success. Instead of softening around the pain of the hotness, you can simply soften around any pain or self-criticism over not "doing the exercise properly."

The Sudden Pain Exercise

We all suffer from sudden pain on occasion: stubbing a toe, dropping a box on the foot, banging the head on the trunk lid of the car. And many of us react with the hit-thumb-throw-hammer syndrome —that's the American way of dealing with unexpected pain. Although it's hard to formulate as an exercise, the next time you experience a *mild* but unexpected physical pain, try to soften around it, just as you did in these last exercises. Refocus your attention onto the breath, drop your shoulders, unclench your fists and jaw.

Of course, it's harder to do when you're not expecting the pain—that's the reason for practicing all of the neural path therapy techniques in controlled experiments before trying to use them in real life. But it's strangely satisfying to soften around the momentary pain of a barked shin or a bumped noggin, even if you can only manage to remember to soften around such a pain once in a while.

Sudden Pain Prep Exercise

You can also visualize a scenario that usually triggers a negative neural path and then visualize practicing a new response to the scenario. As with other exercises in this book, this is the way you can create, then reinforce, a new and improved neural path.

1. Visualize yourself stubbing your toe, bumping your head on that low fixture, or some other likely if unpleasant scenario that might cause you sudden pain. Imagine both the situation and the pain it causes as clearly as possible.

2. Then imagine yourself instantly refocusing your attention onto the breath while consciously relaxing shoulder, stomach, jaw, and hand muscles.

3. Next time you hit your thumb with the hammer, this may help you react by softening, rather than hardening, around the pain. Please note that even if you get mad for a few seconds—even if you curse and throw the hammer down—a belated softening is far better than none at all.

Hit Thumb with Hammer   *Fight or Flight Kicks In*   **Tighten**   THROW HAMMER: CURSE!   *Remember to Soften*   SIGH, MAYBE EVEN COMPASSION RESPONSE?

Perception   *Processing*   OUTPUT   *Processing*   OUTPUT

Exercise for Chronic or Ongoing Physical Pain

This exercise may be useful if you suffer from any kind of chronic or ongoing physical pain. This can include discomfort even as transient as that of a cold or flu.

1. Spend, as usual, a few moments with your favorite breathing exercise.

2. When relaxed, focus your mental attention onto any sensations of physical discomfort, whether they may be back spasms or congested sinuses.

3. If you've worked successfully with the compassion exercises, try to divide your attention between a focus on the compassion response—after all, what better time to feel some compassion for yourself than when you are sick—and the physical symptoms. If you can't muster any compassion, just split your attention between the breath and the symptoms.

4. Notice any self-talk that may arise. Label it briefly ("That's the old this-shouldn't-be-happening-to-me story"). Then return to split focus on the breath (or compassion) and your symptoms.

With practice, this type of exercise will help you to use negative events, mental or physical, to build valuable skills. In step five, we'll elaborate on this concept of weaving straw into gold (or turning manure into fertilizer, as an earthier type might say).

ABOUT MENTAL PAIN

You probably bought this book because you suffer from some kind of mental pain rather than because you have physical pain or a propensity to drop rocks on your toe. As with physical pain, when painful thoughts—or the emotions that they engender—arise, you can blunt their effect by softening, rather than hardening, yourself to them. And as with any action, it's easier to do if you prepare and practice for it.

Mental Pain Prep Exercises

We'd like to teach you how to prepare to face mental pain using a technique that we call *progressive neural desensitization*. The exercises we'll present are simply variations on the split attention exercises that you've already done. But we'd like to take this opportunity to discuss the theoretical underpinnings of this type of work.

Progressive Neural Desensitization

Often, when working with fears or phobias, psychologists teach their clients to use what is called *progressive desensitization*. For example, if a client has a fear of snakes, the therapist will help him into a relaxed state, then show him a very mildly negative stimulus—say, a cartoon of an earthworm. When the client can maintain the relaxed state while looking at the cartoon of an earthworm, the therapist substitutes a picture of an actual earthworm. Progressively more powerful negative stimuli are used as, with practice, the client gets better at maintaining a relaxed state while observing the stimulus object: a cartoon of a cute little snake, a picture of a small snake, a stuffed animal snake toy, a video of a large snake.

The Progressive Neural Desensitization (PND) Process

In progressive neural desensitization, all the work is done in the brain—no pictures, no stuffed snakes. Here's the general process that you'll use to desensitize yourself to painful thoughts, regardless of the specific content of any particular thought. Once you have desensitized yourself to the thought, it will be easier to soften around it.

1. Begin, as usual, with a moment of your favorite breath-focus exercise.

2. Bring the thought of a mildly painful event or memory, a fear for the future, or an unpleasant type of self-talk that you indulge in into your mind.

3. Try to balance your attention between the breath focus and the thought.

4. It's like being on a seesaw: you'll focus too much on the thought and forget the breath, or focus too much on the breath and forget the thought. Just try to stay balanced between the two mental objects.

5. With practice, you'll find that the thought has less power to affect you, to trigger a fight-or-fight response.

6. End the exercise with a moment of conscious softening: shoulders, stomach, jaw, hands. Then, if you can, try to generate a moment of compassion about the pain that you and every other human being are subject to.

This exercise can be applied to virtually any kind of mental pain, whether it derives from a particular thought, a memory, or from the self-talk process.

Prescriptions for Pains

Now we'll say a few words about specific applications for softening around pain. Once you've practiced some split-attention work with those issues that trouble you, you will be able to use the shrug-and-sigh and applet techniques on them, which are described at the end of this chapter.

Pain of Unfulfilled Desire

Splitting attention between the breath and an unfulfilled desire is easy to practice on the level of real life. This is similar to the desire prep exercise of step two. Just take an extra moment or two for a split-attention exercise before you head for the fridge or the bathroom or before you take the credit card from your wallet. To deal with larger or more pressing desires (Should I buy that new sofa? Go to Rio for Carnival?), use the general PND process that you just learned, and put in a few practice sessions before deciding whether to fulfill that particular desire or not, or not for a while...

Pain of Anger or Angst

These two are good subjects for progressive neural desensitization. Make sure you start with mildly painful mental objects—low-level angst or annoyance rather than rage. Just follow the general instructions for the PND process, and it will get easier with practice.

Interpersonal Pain

For many of us, our most acute pains make themselves known in relationships with others. We'll address a few more interpersonal issues in step five, but for now, choose a specific interpersonal issue that troubles you in your relationship with someone, and use the progressive neural desensitization techniques described above to work on softening around it. Begin with a mild one, and work your way up to softening around the more annoying issues that your colleagues, family members, or spouse may present you with. But please, remember the Serenity Prayer—these exercises are not intended to help you deny or avoid changing painful interpersonal problems—only to help you soften around the ones that you either cannot change or choose not to change at the present time.

Pain of Not Being in Control

It's painful to live in a world where any virus or runaway taxi can change or even end our lives. We like to feel as though we are in control, although we know deep inside that we are not. This is one of the most difficult of pains, as it reflects the deep existential pain described in chapter 6. Yet there is a certain satisfaction in being able, once in a while, to admit that we just don't know.

Don't know what will come next. Don't know how we'll deal with it. The phone ring exercise, below, will help you to begin to work with this unavoidable human issue.

The Shrug-and-Sigh Shortcut

After you've spent some time with the compassion and softening-around-pain exercises—that is, developing new neural paths that end with compassion or softening—there's a convenient shortcut that you can develop and use in many situations.

A synecdoche ("sih-*neck*-doh-kee") is a poetic device in which a part is used to represent a larger whole, such as "eight sails were approaching" to indicate the arrival of a windsurfer fleet. Once you've learned to identify and cultivate the sense of compassion and the skill of softening around pain, you can create a synecdoche, or quick representation, to express these subtle and complex concepts instantly.

1. Just tense then relax your shoulders and neck—like a shrug—inhaling as you tense and sighing as you relax.

2. As you sigh, bring a thought of compassion and softness into your mind.

If you practice this simple technique, you'll be able to use it whenever pain arises, whether mental or physical. If the pain continues or comes back, just do it again, as often as you need to.

Applets of the Mind

Applets are little subapplications that are embedded into a program and which run on a computer when other things are happening. They provide limited but useful functions and services and are often set to run automatically when your computer encounters a certain computing situation. If you've practiced the above softening-around-pain PND exercises, you can use them to create mental applets. Like a computer applet, these are simply well-rehearsed mental paths that are created to first detect when a certain situation (such as the pain of desire, or anger) arises, then automatically launch your prepracticed softening-around-pain response (such as a shrug and sigh).

The Softening Applet Exercise

Obviously, as with any neural path, the more you rehearse an applet, the more automatic it becomes and the easier to launch into action.

1. Identify a specific pain stimulus, such as "every time I hear X's voice," or "every time I see a picture of ____."

2. Use the general shrug-and-sigh shortcut to soften around the pain you feel from that stimulus.

3. Visualize yourself using an applet in which the pain stimulus triggers the shrug-and-sigh exercise.

    Practice until it becomes easy to trigger the softening applet whenever the painful stimulus arises. This is an excellent strategy for working with the pain of blaming or judging, by the way.

Phone Ring Control Exercise/Applet

For many people, this variation on a shrug-and-sigh applet is an easy one to start on, since a specific physical cue—a sound—reminds you to start the applet. Every time the phone rings, let it be the alarm of an applet that reminds you that you just ... don't know. This call could be the best news you've had in years, or the worst, or a telemarketer, or a wrong number.

1. Don't pick it up until the end of the third ring.

2. Inhale during each ring, and think something like, "This call could be the best news I've ever gotten."

3. Exhale during each silence between rings, and think something like. "This call could be really bad news." Soften your body as you think this.

Please feel free to create applets of your own using the same general pattern: a specific pain itself is used as a trigger to begin a process that ends with softening and compassion.

Summing Up

If the compassion exercises in step three were difficult for you, you may want to return to them now that you've worked on softening around pain. Please remember that these acceptance techniques in steps three and four are much more subtle and harder to master than the coping skills of the earlier steps, and don't fall into the trap of being hard on yourself for not being soft or compassionate enough.

CHAPTER 5

Step Five

Wise Paths: Putting It All Together

You have now studied all of the elements involved in the neural path therapy method. These include

- Exercises to build mental muscle, so that you can refocus your attention onto the breath at any time, stimulate the R & R response, and short-circuit the fight-or-flight response

- Observation of your own neural neighborhood, with both its useful paths and its dead ends

- The compassion response and the ability to soften around pain

Now it's time to look at the general strategy into which these elements can be combined to form a wiser and more compassionate way of living. Some of the material in this step will be review, and some of it will be new.

PLEASE REMEMBER THAT THE ABILITY TO USE ANY ELEMENT OF THE NEURAL PATH THERAPY METHOD IS CONTINGENT UPON HAVING SUFFICIENT MENTAL MUSCLE TO CONTROL THE FOCUS OF YOUR ATTENTION. SO DON'T FORGET TO PRACTICE YOUR MINI EXERCISES—WHETHER DRAWING A BREATH, COUNTING A BREATH, LABELING A BREATH, OR WALKING AND BREATHING—AT LEAST A FEW TIMES A DAY, EVERY DAY.

THE GENERAL STRATEGY

Here's a summary of the overall strategy of this book:

- Mental muscle gives you the ability to change neural paths: from trigger → emotion, to trigger → breath focus, or to trigger → soften around pain.

- Your understanding of neural paths and of your own neural neighborhood means that in effect you are now acting as your own therapist.

- You are able to observe your own mental patterns objectively, noticing old pathways, trigger thoughts, and self-talk that produce beliefs, biases, transferences, fears, and anger.

- You can become aware of general lifelong tendencies toward angst or anger, toward blaming yourself or others, by observing your self-talk.

- You can treat thoughts as nothing more than mental objects, which you have the power to manipulate. You can anticipate painful or difficult situations and prepare in advance to handle them with skill through coping or acceptance strategies.

- When you do these things, you are *choosing* how to react, and you no longer bring the past into the present in the form of knee-jerk reactions to old pathways.

Using All the Steps at Once

You will often need to use all of the first four steps together— a combination strategy of thought-watching to choose your paths, and mental muscle and breath focus to allow you to navigate them, with compassion for yourself and softening around the pain of not doing it very perfectly.

OVERCOMING OBSTACLES

As in any endeavor, you will encounter obstacles in your path (as well as in your neural paths). We'd like to discuss a few of them, since anticipation of obstacles helps to overcome them.

If You Feel Like Quitting...

We've already discussed the common self-defeating paths of angst and anger that can lead you to give up or quit. Please remember, when you mess up by getting fearful or angry, when you forget to use the program or let it lapse for a while: don't let a slip be the cause of self-sabotage. Let it remain just a slip by remembering that one of the most self-defeating dead-end paths is the one that turns self-hate over a single slip into permanent sabotage of your neural path therapy program!

If You Don't Have Time

With all due respect, if you've already read this far, that's no excuse. Reading this book is the only part of the program that takes any time at all. Using the mini exercises (page 38) lets you integrate your mental muscle practice directly into daily life. And the increased mental clarity and reduced stress that using this method can offer will actually increase the amount of usable time and energy that you have.

The Synecdoche of Pain

Synecdoche has its uses, in poetry and in the shrug-and-sigh exercise in step four. But many of us use a form of it in a negative way—we let the neighbor's barking dog that wakes us up one morning become the personification, the representative synecdoche, of every dog that has ever frightened or hounded us! Don't allow a single rejection to bring up the pain of every rejection that you have ever faced. Recognizing this common pattern in your life—in advance—will help you to be prepared to soften around the issue and apply lots of compassion when it arises.

The Sins of the Fathers (and Mothers)

Therapy is a good place in which to analyze your childhood and your relations with parents. But lying beneath the specifics of your upbringing, the fact is that the most well-meaning and loving parents often manage to forget that even very young children are people, with needs and feelings that matter to the child. Almost all of us have suffered from the loneliness and emptiness that comes from being treated as an object. It happens first when our needs are not understood ("No, you huge fools! I want a clean diaper, not a bottle!"). It happens later when we recognize that our parents have "empty spots" inside themselves that they need us to fill, and we begin to believe that we must behave in certain ways to fill those voids and thus obtain parental love. The fact that our parents did this to us because their parents did it to them may help us with forgiveness (see below) but not with the pain that this early objectification can help to cause.

This process is probably the genesis of our "shoulds"—the belief that we "should" act or be a certain way, which is the first step to the objectification of ourselves by ourselves. We begin to value ourselves on what we produce, how we look, who we hang out with, rather than on who we are inside. Many therapists believe that this original pain is the beginning of much angst or anger in later life. It's a big pain to apply compassion toward and soften around, but recognizing it as an issue (if it is, for you) is a good and necessary start.

INTERPERSONAL OBSTACLES

Even when we have gotten our own neural neighborhood relatively well mapped and navigated, we may have problems with interpersonal relationships. Some hints on working with these follow:

- Know how your own neural paths (including beliefs, transference, and so on) affect your relationships.

- Remember that the other person has neural pathways too. Can you see some of his or hers? Can you begin to map out which paths are the other person's and which are yours? Which of his or her paths are triggered by your paths?

- Watch your self-talk. Do you attribute motivations to others by thinking "You are always trying to bug me," rather than simply observing "You are tapping your foot while I try to read." Do you have "shoulds" for others' behavior? (For example, "He shouldn't leave me to be with his friends.")

- Soften around the interpersonal pain of others not being as you wish they were.

- Try to develop a sense of compassion toward others while protecting yourself physically or mentally if necessary.

- Practice the split-attention interpersonal exercises on pages 79 through 81 and use them to defuse anger and fear when you are with difficult people or in difficult interpersonal situations.

OBSTACLES AND THE MASTER SKILL

Imagine a downhill skier who sticks to flat terrain or a white-water kayaker who stays only on the lake. Sure, the beginning skier starts with the bunny slopes, and the beginning kayaker practices her basic skills in a pond or even a swimming pool. But soon, it's the steeper slopes and whirling rapids that both provide the reason for the sport and improve the abilities of the athlete. Likewise, if you use the act of dealing with the obstacles in your life as a means to build mental muscle and practice acceptance, you have spun straw into gold, made manure into fertilizer.

Summing Up

Please accept our congratulations on making it this far. We know from our clients and from our own lives that the attempt to live with awareness and acceptance is difficult but satisfying. We can only reiterate, once again, that your efforts are noble and that your "failures" should be rewarded with compassion and softening around pain rather than reacted to with anger or angst. When you feel ready, please go on to chapter 6, Beyond the Steps.

Beyond the Steps: The Path to Total Freedom

Steps one and two were concerned with the level of *coping*, of dealing with the issues of daily life by changing them, or changing our relationship to them. Steps three and four were concerned with the level of *acceptance*, of dealing with mental or physical pain through compassion and softening. But there are levels that lie higher and deeper than that.

In this chapter, we'll take a quick look at ways of bringing happiness and meaning into life and then at ways of transcending the body, brain, or sense of self—and look at what may lie beyond. These levels have been the subject of perhaps a hundred thousand books—religious, spiritual, and philosophical. But even the content of these few pages may give you a hint on the direction in which to turn your mental attention in order to explore the human experience in its full depth and glory.

HAPPINESS AND MEANING

"Happiness" and "meaning": these two words might not seem to go together, since for many people, the definition of "happiness" may likely differ from their definition of "meaning in life," if they have one at all. Yet increasing amounts of research indicate that the elements usually thought to increase happiness—winning the lottery, health, sexual satisfaction—have little positive effect. Instead, people who say that they find meaning in their lives—from a job, a hobby, or a charitable endeavor, for example, tend to rate themselves as happier than those who don't have such positive experiences. A growing body of literature indicates, unsurprisingly, that doing altruistic acts (on the level of five a week) makes people happier (Lyubomirsky, Sheldon, and Schkade, forthcoming). The literature also indicates that writing down a few things that make you happy each day can increase your level of happiness.

What You See Is What You Get

We believe that this is simply a function of what we've been saying all along. Where you focus your mental attention has a profound effect on every aspect of your life. Consider writing down, or mentally listing, at least three things a day that you are grateful for. Keeping such a journal forces you to focus mental attention on good things, rather than on complaints or old grudges, or the ways in which the world should treat you but doesn't. And what you focus attention on, you strengthen the neural path to. So if you spend some time each day focusing on good things, you will remember (have stronger neural path connections to) good things, and you'll be happier.

Compassion in Action

As part of your practice of developing compassion, you might visit a nursing home or a shut-in neighbor. While visiting with them, just follow your breath. Or even better, follow theirs, since the shared-breath exercise (page 99) is a very powerful compassion evoker. Recognizing the loneliness of another's life can be a great opportunity for compassion, aimed at both yourself and others.

Forgiveness

Letting go of old resentments improves your neural neighborhood immensely, so this is a good reason to emphasize forgiveness over judging or blaming (no matter how satisfying it may seem to be right). Whether applied to yourself or to another, it is more important and useful to understand an event or behavior (perhaps using the interpersonal hints from step five) than to judge it or to blame yourself or others for it. If judging or blaming is a problem for you, it might be well worth creating an applet (as on pages 114 and 115) to help work on those issues.

Historic Focus on What's Not Right

Of course, it's often easier to focus on what's *not* right, and with good reason. Since our earliest ancestors crawled from the ocean onto the beach—if not before—it was imperative for them to focus on what was wrong rather than what was right. The single ripple in the grass, indicating a hidden predator, was far more important to pay attention to than the thousands of acres of beautiful but unmoving savannah.

Modern Focus on What's Not Right

This focus on what's not right continues today. Our media (which is simply an electronic extension of our five perceptual senses) is filled with images of war, pain, need, and murder. The average middle-class American child—who might never witness more actual violence than a few fistfights, if that—sees tens of thousands of acts of violence before reaching adulthood.

Cultural Focus on What's Not Right

It's also important to remember that for quite a while (some would say since the agricultural revolution many thousands of years ago, while others would date this from the industrial revolution a mere couple hundred years past), our culture has tended to value us more for what we produce than for who we are inside. With the advent of a mass media based on sales of objects and services, the objectification of *Homo sapiens* was complete. Commercial advertising tells us that we are not okay as we are and must buy products to make us more beautiful, less fat, better smelling. We should have the right car, house, spouse. We compare ourselves to the rich and beautiful people that we see on TV rather than to our peers and neighbors, and we feel small and impoverished in comparison, no matter how materially secure we may be in this world of want.

Existential Pain

As though there were not enough personal, historical, and cultural pain in everyday life, there is a higher level of pain that people often deny. This is sometimes called "existential pain"—the pain of understanding that existence is limited, and that we, and all that we love, must come to an end. Most people try to avoid thinking about this type of pain. Yet this pain is a uniquely human experience, since only humans have enough self-awareness to know that they must die.

WHAT CAN BE DONE?

We can try to maximize our focus on compassionate actions and on being grateful when appropriate and try to minimize, without denial, our focus on painful stimuli (entertaining and addictive though it may be, violent media gives us little of real benefit). And with all painful issues, understanding and anticipating their presence can help us to soften around them, when they do occur in either mental or physical reality.

There are two more things we can do. We can try to encourage benevolent cycles, rather than vicious ones, into our life. And we can try—either through religious or spiritual means—to transcend for a moment the limited body/brain/self that so often seems to be all that we are.

Vicious Cycles, Benevolent Cycles

We've all heard of the vicious cycle, in which two elements interact to simultaneously worsen each other. In the vicious cycle of anger, our anger contracts and narrows our awareness—all we can see is anger. And the more tightly awareness is focused on the anger, the more angry we become. Fear multiplies itself in the same way.

In the benevolent cycle of compassion and understanding, the more you understand—of yourself, and of others—the easier it is to be compassionate and to soften around pain (including the pain of anger or fear). And the more compassionate and able to soften around pain you are, the easier it is to be deeply aware of yourself and of others.

The State of Compassionate Awareness

In the state of compassion and understanding—as during a successful compassion or shared-breath exercise—the heart is open and there is no self-talk. We are conscious and aware, but the mind, for a moment, is not telling stories. There may also be some identification with all living creatures, all of whom must age and die just as we do.

We might say that the state of coping—the state of step one and step two—is the state of "I am _____": "I am angry." "I am fearful." We are aware of the self, with its needs, its neural paths, its foibles and frailties. But in the state of acceptance, compassion, and understanding, we might say that we are in the state of simply "I am." We are aware, we are experiencing the state of compassion, but we are not actually thinking, and certainly not thinking of ourselves.

Transcendent States

In the state of compassionate awareness, we move from a focus on specific states of our individual body/self ("I am hungry," and so on) to a more generalized awareness that we might express as "I am" plus sense of compassion (that's your combination of awareness—or "am-ness"—and compassion). In a transcendent state, we lessen the focus on the individual self, so that "I am" becomes simply "am." For a moment, we are not particularly identified with our individual body and personal history as held in our brain. We'll discuss the sense of "am-ness" more on page 134.

This subtle and (sadly) rather rare state of awareness is usually experienced in a spiritual context of communion with God (if connected with a particular religion) or communion with the universe or universal consciousness (if not connected with a particular religion). It may be that the widespread human desire to be part of something larger than oneself (which so often expresses itself in sports team affiliation and identification with idols of many sorts) is a pale and distorted reflection of the craving for the transcendent state.

Enhancing the Experience of Prayer

For those of us belonging to the Christian, Jewish, or Muslim religion, it may be useful to think of the conscious mind—when filled with fears, angers, and desires—as a screen between the individual and God. If so, it's clear that removing that screen may well enhance the ability to communicate with the Deity. And removing the screen of the mind is what helps us enter into a transcendent state of prayer, a state of communion with God.

To experiment with this is simple, although not easy.

1. Work with the neural path therapy method for long enough so that your mental attention spends more time focused on the R & R response and on compassion than it does on anger, fear, bitterness, or other top ten–type thoughts that usually cloud our consciousness.

2. Then, before engaging in prayer, spend a few minutes doing breath-focus exercises, followed by compassion focus.

If this concept appeals to you, a modern edition of the earliest-known and classic Christian work on the contemplative tradition, *The Cloud of Unknowing* (Johnston 1973) may be useful.

Transcendence Without Religion

The same process just described can be used in a nonreligious context. After completing the first part, which might take a few weeks, months, or years, you can spend a few minutes on the breath focus and compassion focus. Then turn your mental attention to the sense of "I am" that resides at the very base of your consciousness. Consider that "I am sad" or "I am happy" are transient states, but that the "I am" sense that you had as a child is precisely the same as the "I am" sense you experience right now. It's a sense of conscious presence, which is hard to describe but eminently real.

Some find it useful to trace states of consciousness from simpler to more complex. For example, animals clearly exist and certainly have awareness—they perceive events and act on their perceptions (watch a frog eat a bug). Humans are aware that they have thought processes; that's what self-awareness is about, as we've covered so extensively in the coping steps of this book. But only a few people stop to think about the nature of awareness itself. You are one of them, so please spend a few short sessions mulling the nature of the "I am" sense.

When you feel ready for the next step, consider the "I" part of the "I am." Does it refer to your body? Your brain? Your personality? Your set of neural paths? Your personal history?

Those who practice this type of exercise with diligence often find that the "I" can be separated to some extent from the "am." A sense of "am-ness" itself can be identified, and many find that recognizing this am-ness provides a feeling of direct communion with God, the universal consciousness, the all-that-is. It becomes clear to them, for a moment at least, that am-ness is what connects all life. As with any exercise in this book, if this exercise is difficult, frustrating, or causes pain, please treat yourself not with criticism but with the compassion that you would give to a dear friend or a small child in need, and which you—we all—so richly deserve.

The Life of Meaning and the Meaning of Life

Perhaps the real meaning of life is that our current existence on Earth provides us with the opportunity to learn that we are more than our neural paths, our personal history, our brain, our mind, ourselves as the objects that our parents, our culture, our biology has made us. An essential part of this task might then be to override the animal-based mind with its billion-year history by learning to consciously control our neural pathways. Another part might be to overcome the existential pain that only humans can know—the pain that makes some close down in a vicious cycle of fear, anger, and contracted awareness—with the goal of seeking a benevolent cycle of wider and deeper compassion and awareness, in spite of all obstacles.

If this is our task, it's clear that we need to be less concerned with "things" and self-image. Rather, we need only to be aware, compassionate people—not rich, not beautiful, not even well liked by others—although being sincerely cherished by others is more likely to happen if we are aware and compassionate.

Aware and compassionate humans are also more likely to treat the earth that bears us with care and respect. More likely to be generous with and protective of the most vulnerable members of our race: the very old and the young. More likely to face the great challenges of our awful and awe-full world with joy and humor rather than with despair and bitterness.

To go back to the opening words of this book, these goals are only possible if we are able to relate to the brain not as a tyrant, but as a wonderful servant who supports us in our missions, instead of forcing us to waste our precious time, energy, and resources on unimportant or counterproductive old pathways, traveled by habit instead of choice.

A FEW WORDS OF GRATITUDE

We thank you for the gift of your attention. Without that great and important gift, these words are nothing more than meaningless dark marks on a white page. We hope that this book will help you to continue giving that greatest of gifts, to your friends, your family, your loved ones, and most of all, to yourself.

APPENDIX A

Continuation of the R & R Exercise

4. Stay with the image of your least favorite person for two or three more seconds.

5. Now, without delay, focus your attention carefully on the following draw-a-breath chart, and breathe along with it:

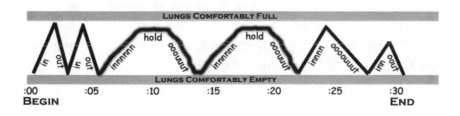

The question now is, What happened to the thought of your least favorite person? For most of us, simply refocusing our attention onto the breath almost instantly eradicates the LFP thought, and reading the draw-a-breath chart for even five or ten seconds more is enough to reverse the effects of the fight-or-flight response.

Refocus and Relax

In the little R & R demonstration you just completed, moving from the LFP image to the draw-a-breath chart probably had a profound and immediate effect on your mental state. Two interrelated factors were involved. The first is that simply refocusing your attention is often enough to cut short a fight-or-flight response and the emotion it engenders. The second is that refocusing attention onto the breathing process stimulates the relax-and-release response (which then reverses the effects of the fight-or-flight response).

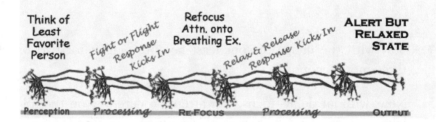

But focusing attention onto the breath isn't just useful for dealing with unwanted or unuseful emotions—it's also a great way to build mental muscle.

Now please go back to page 26, and continue reading with the section entitled "Breathing and Mental Muscle."

Continuation of the Thought Versus Reality (TVSR) Exercise

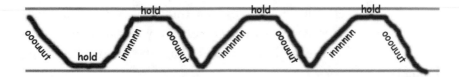

Did you have a moment of indecision or surprise when you saw this chart and realized that it started on an exhale, rather than the inhale? Perhaps you even indulged in an accidental microsecond of breathing in. This would not be surprising, since, so far, all of the draw-a-breath charts have started with an in-breath.

In neural path terms, you've already created a neural path for following a draw-a-breath chart. And although you are probably not *consciously* aware of it, this path probably includes the element of emptying your lungs as you prepare to begin breathing along with the chart. Thus, when you turned to the previous page, you were actually paying attention to your fantasy—your expectation or your thought about what was going to happen—rather than the reality of the actual chart.

We're not monsters or martinets. We don't care if you mess up a fraction of a second of a breath chart. But the ramifications of this exercise are important, since it shows that sometimes when you believe that you are paying attention to physical, external reality, you may really be paying attention to your *thoughts* about reality.

CONFUSING REALITY WITH THOUGHTS ABOUT REALITY

You're driving along a boring stretch of the freeway at seventy miles per hour. Of course the car in front of you is going to keep going at the same speed. But a dog or a deer or a broken muffler in the road slows him down abruptly, and bam!—a fender bender. You are paying attention to *thoughts* about the driving, not the actual, changing conditions.

Your coworker Mary is a great, low-maintenance friend. Cheerful, competent, and stable. One day, Mary comes in, and she's dragging just a little; perhaps something not so good has happened at home. Do you even notice? Or are you paying attention to your *mental image* of Mary, rather than the living, breathing human being?

"I'm just not musical [or good at math, or athletic, or articulate]," you say. And when an opportunity arises to explore this belief—a friend gives you a harmonica or invites you to try playing racketball with her—you avoid the opportunity. You are paying attention to your *beliefs* about yourself, not the reality of who you are or who you could become.

If you don't investigate your thoughts by thought watching and control them by neural navigation, you risk allowing your thoughts to control you. When you can observe your thoughts, you can then gain some control over them by choosing your own neural paths, rather than simply following habitual ones.

Now please return to page 56, and continue reading.

References

Harp, D. 1996. *The New Three Minute Meditator.* Oakland, Calif.: New Harbinger.

Johnston, W., ed. *The Cloud of Unknowing.* 1973. *New York: Doubleday.*

Lyubomirsky, S., K. M. Sheldon, and D. Schkade. Forthcoming. Pursuing happiness: The architecture of sustainable change. *Review of General Psychology.*

About the Neural Path Therapy Web Site

We've created the Web site www.neuralpaththerapy.com as a way of providing additional useful information on using the neural path method to best advantage. This Web site provides

- Instructions and advice for therapists using this method with clients

- An e-mail discussion group for individuals using this method

- Instructions on how using the method with another person can make it easier and more effective, and a buddy bulletin board to help visitors find an online buddy to do the program with

• Suggestions for use of the method in the workplace

We will attempt to answer frequently asked questions posted in the e-mail discussion group.

About David's Corporate Work

Since 1998, David has been using, testing, and refining the concepts of neural path therapy in his corporate workshops and *pro bono* events. Since the desired result of NPT is so broad — learning to use that great tool, the human brain, more effectively — the range of events that David can offer is similarly wide. A few of his most commonly requested presentations include:

- Misery Loves Companies: Dealing with Negativity in the Workplace™

- Mental Muscle: How a Strong Mind will Get Your Through a Weak Economy™

- Alert and Aware: How to See It Coming, Before It Hits the Fan™

- How to Stay Focused When All Heck is Breaking Loose™

- MOJO Work: Maintaining Mindfulness On the JOb

However, these are not "canned" speeches. Rather, David customizes each presentation after studying the needs and issues facing the group (and, if appropriate, issues facing the general trade in which that group is involved).

David demonstrating the use of the Draw-A-Breath chart for a group composed of 1200 school board presidents.

For example, in an event for the Kraft Foods New Product Division, David created a workshop on enhancing creativity by teaching participants to notice the neural paths that tend to make "left-brained" participants want to end the brainstorming process prematurely. In an event for hospice personnel, David helped attendees to notice Dead End Paths that exacerbate burnout, and which can be combated by a healthy dose of compassion and softening around pain. In a session for Merck Pharmaceutical's salespeople, he concentrated on the neural paths that reduce stress and increase focus during "cold call" situations. And for a workshop on Peak Communication™ during crisis situations for an international symposium sponsored by the FBI, David trained participants to short-circuit the fight or flight response and re-focus on maintaining interpersonal communication skills.

A small group of attendees focus with great intensity on David's instructions.

Applying Neural Path Therapy techniques to workplace situations may be innovative enough for some. But David's workshops take innovation to a whole new level, since the tool with which he teaches NPT is ... the blues harmonica! It may just be the most joyful, creative, and entertaining way ever to teach people to gain control over the human mind!

For more information on exactly how David uses the harmonica to teach Neural Path Therapy to corporate or non-profit groups, please visit www.davidharp.com.

Some Other
New Harbinger Titles

Angry All the Time, Item 3929 $13.95

Handbook of Clinical Psychopharmacology for Therapists, 4th edition, Item 3996 $55.95

Writing For Emotional Balance, Item 3821 $14.95

Surviving Your Borderline Parent, Item 3287 $14.95

When Anger Hurts, 2nd edition, Item 3449 $16.95

Calming Your Anxious Mind, Item 3384 $12.95

Ending the Depression Cycle, Item 3333 $17.95

Your Surviving Spirit, Item 3570 $18.95

Coping with Anxiety, Item 3201 $10.95

The Agoraphobia Workbook, Item 3236 $19.95

Loving the Self-Absorbed, Item 3546 $14.95

Transforming Anger, Item 352X $10.95

Don't Let Your Emotions Run Your Life, Item 3090 $17.95

Why Can't I Ever Be Good Enough, Item 3147 $13.95

Your Depression Map, Item 3007 $19.95

Successful Problem Solving, Item 3023 $17.95

Working with the Self-Absorbed, Item 2922 $14.95

The Procrastination Workbook, Item 2957 $17.95

Coping with Uncertainty, Item 2965 $11.95

The BDD Workbook, Item 2930 $18.95

You, Your Relationship, and Your ADD, Item 299X $17.95

The Stop Walking on Eggshells Workbook, Item 2760 $18.95

Conquer Your Critical Inner Voice, Item 2876 $15.95

The PTSD Workbook, Item 2825 $17.95

Call **toll free, 1-800-748-6273,** or log on to our online bookstore at **www.newharbinger.com** to order. Have your Visa or Mastercard number ready. Or send a check for the titles you want to New Harbinger Publications, Inc., 5674 Shattuck Ave., Oakland, CA 94609. Include $4.50 for the first book and 75¢ for each additional book, to cover shipping and handling. (California residents please include appropriate sales tax.) Allow two to five weeks for delivery.

Prices subject to change without notice.